John Hritzuk has been a professor of educational psychology at the University of Calgary in Alberta, Canada, for fifteen years. In addition to extensive traveling and lecturing, he has conducted special workshops on loneliness.

PRENTICE-HALL INTERNATIONAL, INC., London
PRENTICE-HALL OF AUSTRALIA PTY. LIMITED, Sydney
PRENTICE-HALL CANADA INC., Toronto
PRENTICE-HALL OF INDIA PRIVATE LIMITED, New Delhi
PRENTICE-HALL OF JAPAN, INC., Tokyo
PRENTICE-HALL OF SOUTHEAST ASIA PTE. LTD., Singapore
WHITEHALL BOOKS LIMITED, Wellington, New Zealand

JOHN HRITZUK

THE SILENT COMPANY

*How to Deal
With Loneliness*

A SPECTRUM BOOK

Prentice-Hall, Inc., Englewood Cliffs, N.J. 07632

Library of Congress Cataloging in Publication Data

Hritzuk, John (date)
    The silent company.

    "A Spectrum Book"
    Bibliography: p.
    Includes index.
    1. Loneliness.   2. Men—Psychology.   I. Title.
BF575.L7H74 1982   158'.2   82-10176
ISBN 0-13-809822-0
ISBN 0-13-809814-X (pbk.)

On page 93 appears the article
"I'm So Lonely . . . Will Someone Call Me?"
by William Endicott, *Los Angeles Times*, November 26, 1970.
Copyright, 1970, *Los Angeles Times*.
It is reprinted by permission.

A SPECTRUM BOOK

Printed in the United States of America

10 9 8 7 6 5 4 3 2 1

ISBN 0-13-809822-0

ISBN 0-13-809814-X (PBK.)

Editorial/production supervision by Chris McMorrow
Cover design by Jeannette Jacobs
Cover illustration by Jim Kinstrey
Manufacturing buyer: Cathie Lenard

This Spectrum Book is available to businesses and organizations
at a special discount when ordered in large quantities.
For information, contact Prentice-Hall, Inc.,
General Publishing Division, Special Sales,
Englewood Cliffs, N.J. 07632.

to
Natasha, Irene, and Alex Hritzuk

but
especially to all people
who struggle with loneliness

Contents

Foreword

Loneliness has been described as our number one national disease and rightly so. The tentacles of loneliness creep into every age group: The teenager buffeted by the storms of physical and emotional change, insecure relationships, and fears for the future contemplates suicide and all too often carries it through. The middle-aged feel that life is slipping by without those dreamed-about grand achievements being realized. The older years are when the song "Is That All There Is?" takes on a poignant significance, and death is indeed peering around the corner. That's the time when, as an elderly friend of mine says, "You may know all the answers, but nobody asks you the questions."

Our society has made loneliness a billion dollar business. It is catered to by social agencies, singles bars, package tours, lonely hearts clubs, and massage parlors. Loneliness is real! It's an ache in the gut, hot tears, psychosomatic illness, deterioration, and early death. It's a feeling of uselessness, hopelessness, insecurity, and naked fear. In *The Silent Company: How to Deal with Loneliness* John Hritzuk has taken us step by step through our lonely worlds, but he has done it with warmth, compassion, and humor.

All of us experience loneliness in varying degrees at certain times during our lives. It is a natural side effect of living. The way we treat our loneliness is the key. It can be a creative, enriching experience, helping us to understand ourselves, revealing who we are, and reflecting our inner selves. But all too often it is destructive and debilitating.

In an interview I did in London, England, for "Man Alive" with Metropolitan Anthony Bloom of the Russian Orthodox Church, he told me:

> People have lost the ability to communicate. They have lost the ability to express themselves because vocabulary has become shallow, because images have become conventional, because no real attempt is made for an expression of interior experience in adequate words. At the receiving end, understanding has also become shallow because people are afraid of commitment. When a sick person, being asked, "How are you?" answers "All right, thank you!" we don't want to hear anymore. We don't look into the eyes of that person; we don't see the anguish; we don't hear the tremor of the voice; we don't see the obvious signs of disease or the covering lie. To see and hear means to become committed. And we have become timid. We are prepared to establish promiscuous relationships that do not last, but not love relationships that are forever.

The result is that people are lonely because they know perfectly well that they will be dropped at the moment when they are too difficult or superfluous or no longer interesting. I think this is a very important feature of our time—fear of commitment and the inability to communicate either by expressing one's self or by being attentive to what the other person has to say.

We are social animals. We want and need the company, the contact, the approval of others. If, when we reach out, no one is there or our efforts to touch are rebuffed, too often we are plunged into the dark well of loneliness.

One of the best antidotes to the lonely condition is a warm, understanding friend. John Hritzuk, through *The Silent Company: How to Deal with Loneliness*, helps fill that role admirably.

ROY BONISTEEL

Preface

Few people are able to avoid the sting of loneliness in their lives. For some, loneliness lingers for brief, intense hours or days, whereas for others it lingers through endless months and years. Loneliness is a large part of our struggle on this earth.

There are many reasons for our loneliness. Sometimes we are so caught up in our busy lives that we never seem to find time to look at who we are and who we think we are. Yet we still find time to buy, sell, invest, worry, criticize, and blame others for our shortcomings. We worry about food and shelter, but we fail to stress the importance of affection and praise. It is hardly any wonder that loneliness strikes so many people. Sometimes we yearn for another person with whom we can share our lives, but in the end we may find ourselves isolated and lonely. We give many answers, but they do not always fit the right questions. Sometimes we are afraid to look into our lives and accept what we see.

My basic premise is that loneliness, the silent company, begins within each of us. I believe it is important and essential that we be able to enjoy our own company, to like who we are, to exist as unique individuals, and to enjoy some aloneness. When we reach the stage at which we are confident, think well of ourselves, and feel that we are worthy individuals, we are able to conquer Loneliness I. We are then ready to reach out to others and form relationships. We need other people who are meaningful in our lives. If we have no quality in a relationship, we suffer from Loneliness II. Most of us know two people who live together and yet are lonely, desperate souls. Material goods, money, partners, and children are not always the answer to loneliness. We must first grow as individuals and reach new heights before we are ready to share our lives. When two people achieve similar levels of conquering Loneliness I, they are capable of a relationship in which Loneliness II is absent.

Loneliness knows no barriers. Famous, wealthy people succumb to loneliness as well as the insignificant poor. However, in our society, loneliness may be more prevalent during certain stages of the lifespan. For example, adolescence is usually a lonely period. Suicide is the second most common cause of death among adolescents. Adults who are associated with adolescents must be sensitive to the needs of young people. Next, because of the increase in separation and divorce, many older individuals experience lonely times when they are thrust into the world of singles. Misery does not always seek company. Finally, old age with all its aches and pains is no time for great rejoicing. Sometimes the golden years rust very rapidly. There are too many pensioners who feel unloved and unwanted.

There is no simple remedy or recipe for a life free of loneliness. Some of the usual advice that we hear may be the answer to our problems. For example, it is said that we forget about loneliness when we are busy, but what happens when the "busyness" ceases? How can we remain active all the time? In the last two chapters of this book I present a number of exercises that can be a start on the right path to conquering the silent company. We make a healthy beginning when we can admit our loneliness to ourselves and others. We have problems when we are the most lonely souls on this earth and yet pretend that we have the world by the tail.

Writing on the subject of loneliness is in itself a terribly lonely experience. It is not an easy theme to deal with. I discovered that putting one's thoughts on paper involves risking, sharing one's private world with others. Throughout the book I have attempted to take a humanistic approach to the problem of loneliness. We are unique, important people in this world; we must learn to care for ourselves as well as others. These are the long steps we must take if we are to begin the good life.

I wish to thank my close friends who listened to my ideas and who encouraged me to write and share with others. I especially wish to thank Roy Bonisteel, of "Man Alive," CBC-TV, who not only inspired me with his concern for man, but also wrote the foreword.

Prologue

It is autumn. I look out the window; the trees stand tall and silent. The sky is heavy and the rain is falling. I watch the leaves fall, not with a bright, slow flutter, but heavy with rain, quickly and silently. I stare into space; another season, another year.

I think about life. Once it was new, bursting forth in the warmth and light, chasing clouds and moonbeams. There was a proud time when the head was held high, the smile was broad, and the body actually tingled with life.

One day dark clouds appeared on the horizon. The warmth ceased; the wind was cool. I was alone. I felt a stillness in my body. I was drifting in a sea of loneliness. I was afraid.

I have the melancholy feeling again. I do not feel the warmth of the sun or the softness of the air. There are no flowers to enhance the feeling. The raindrops streak down the window pane. Like giant tears on a child's face, they flow incessantly. I can almost hear my heart beat. Why do I feel the way I do? Is it because I am alone? Is it because the warm days of summer are coming to an end? I feel different from everyone in the entire world. My shoulders are burdened with a heavy load. The loneliness gnaws at my heart; it pierces my body and mind.

Will this rain never stop? Will the clouds never roll away? I remember how blue the sky once was. I remember how one looked toward the horizon and saw forever. There were days when my feelings were so high I wanted to paint across the top of the world!

But there is no big sky; there is very little light. A moment seems like an hour. Do others sometimes feel the way I do? Am I the only lonely creature on this earth? Am I really different from others? The silence pierces my ears. The tears flow and the rain continues to fall.

one
Why Study Loneliness?

For many of us, loneliness can be a strange and frightening experience. We usually do not want to admit our lonely feelings, nor do we want to discuss them with others. Many of us experience lonely times, but we have difficulty expressing our feelings in words. Most of us have felt alone and lonely, stripped of meaningful human relationships. We drift in a sea of humanity looking for an anchor. In the meantime we experience the fear, the anxiety, and the quiet heartbeat of loneliness.

Many poems have been written about man's loneliness. There are songs that express the haunting, lonely feeling of people. A photograph can say more than many words: a lonely man whose eyes reflect the emptiness of his soul.

Many of us do not want to get close to our loneliness. We devote a great deal of time and energy avoiding it; we often attempt to disguise it. To deny our loneliness is often a futile experience. We can suppress it, momentarily escape from it, but when the moments pass, the loneliness is still present. We again feel the pain and the fear. We can be in a crowd, yet feel incredibly lonely. We can lose ourselves in music, but loneliness continues to stare at us. We can return home after a concert, a play, or a movie, but loneliness awaits us at the front door. We may attempt to drown our feelings in martinis, but when the party is over, loneliness stares into our eyes from the bottom of the glass. We can be wealthy, beautiful, and powerful, or humble and insignificant, but like death, loneliness does not strike in any predetermined order. We may love or hate, laugh or cry, but loneliness may linger like some silent company.

In the space of two days, I recall seeing several examples of lonely people. While having coffee in a restaurant, I remember four people sitting at the table next to me. The two children were eating silently, while the mother was mechanically stabbing the food on her plate. Father, who had eaten his meal in record-breaking time, was hidden behind a newspaper. He occasionally blew clouds of cigar smoke into the air. No one spoke a word, no one smiled. I saw a teenage girl sitting cross-legged on a cold sidewalk. She leaned against a building and stared at her well-worn sneakers. Her face was immobile; her eyes remained motionless. Like a runaway child, she was alone and so lonely. Thoughts ran through my mind. Why should such a young person be subjected to the cruel, lonely world at such a tender age? I remember seeing an old man, perhaps seventy years of age, sitting on a bench. His trousers were too short, his jacket too long. He sat alone and stared at a window display. His stare seemed to go beyond space itself. I remember one of several meetings I attended with colleagues. A number of people sat around a table playing verbal games. The communication bounced like billiard balls. Individuals were always on guard for fear of being taken by the next person. I often wonder if all meetings are alike. I often wonder if we all experience the same type of loneliness.

How well I remember my own lonely times. How lonely I felt when I left home to attend college. Suddenly I was in a strange world so unlike the quiet, secure life I was used to. Two hundred miles from home seemed like the other side of the world. There were no family or friends. I was sad, lonely, and afraid. I remember teaching in a remote, rural school. How lonely I felt in the evening! There was no phone, no car, and even the nearest farm house was two miles away. At night every creak in the darkness was amplified by my nervous system. How could I forget 1959? I decided to change my environment by accepting a teaching position near the Pacific Ocean. I spent many lonely hours in my two-room apartment, gazing at the ocean, the clouds, and the incessant rain. I can still hear Andy Williams singing "Lonely Street"; the song literally became my anthem. How many times have I kept company with loneliness. Over the years I have tried to run away from it; sometimes I tried to ignore it. However, there were times when I was too exhausted to flee. I tried to experience loneliness, to accept its company, and to deal with all the feelings.

Can I really conquer loneliness? Just when I pick myself up, dust myself off, and begin the upward climb, I again feel the world slipping under my feet. I fall, hard and fast. Tired and dazed, I start living all over again. What is life all about, anyway?

ANALYZING LONELINESS: OBJECTIVES

However, my purpose in writing is not to give you examples of my loneliness or the loneliness of others, nor is it to give you lists of statistics comparing the number of lonely carpenters with the number of lonely housewives. I do not wish to give you the results of surveys of interviews with twenty lonely people. Furthermore, I do not wish to present stories of famous, lonely people or quote from "Ann Landers" or "Dear Abby."

Basically, I have several objectives in mind. One objective is to describe loneliness as it exists in our society and why it exists. There is merit in sharing, discussing, and evaluating ideas instead of denying and avoiding them. Sometimes when we are truly alone in our moments of despair, we feel as if we are the only ones experiencing the fear and the pain of loneliness. We ask, "Why was I chosen to suffer?" "Am I the only one who feels so low?" One must be careful of logic and solutions. I once heard a man say that when he flew he really wasn't afraid, because if the plane crashed he wouldn't be the only one to go down.

There is little comfort in knowing that other lonely people exist around you. We should be able to talk about being alone and being lonely. We should be aware of the value of peace, quiet, and solitude. All of us need a time when we can think and reflect. To be by oneself is a necessary experience. We need time for ourselves, to ponder our very existence. We can examine our world, who we think we are, and who we really feel we are. We need time to grow, to develop our "selves." We cannot expect others to do the growing for us. Being alone does not necessarily mean being lonely.

Loneliness is not always a negative experience. Although it can be associated with a very unpleasant psychological state, being lonely and especially being able to face and truly experience loneliness can be positive. Because of loneliness we may become somewhat different from what we were before. We may be a little stronger, a little wiser, and a little better able to cope with life.

A second objective is to gain a better understanding of human behavior. Why do some people run away from loneliness while others attempt to cope? How do people escape or cope with loneliness? How capable are you of coping with lonely hours? Sometimes we blame everybody but ourselves. We human beings have some very basic, common needs. It is possible to look at these needs in terms of ourselves, and attempt to establish some level of human functioning. Awareness of needs may not be a cure for loneliness, but it can help us understand why we feel and behave the way we do.

Another objective is to examine some of the stages a person passes through in life, and determine which stages are more susceptible to loneliness. As we wander through the maze of life, we experience obstacles that impede our social and emotional growth. We may experience intense loneliness during turbulent periods in a lifetime when we fall and cry. We can hope to be able to rise, laugh, feel and grow again. Adolescence is a particular stage in life when loneliness can strike with full force. The trauma of falling in and out of love is usually accompanied by various degrees of loneliness. Midlife, with marriage breakdown and the resulting disintegration of the family unit, can be an extremely lonely time. Finally, old age is for many the most intensely lonely time. Unlike the other lonely stages in life, many people in old age are unable to cope with the sadness, hopelessness, and pain accompanying their lives. Some wait for eternal sleep to end their painful existence.

The last objective concerns coping with loneliness. The answer is not to escape, ignore, or suppress a lonely feeling. Furthermore, the usual advice to keep busy and active is not always the best solution for the lonely person. We all must take responsibility for our own actions. We must honestly assess our values, philosophy, and even our reasons for existence. We cannot expect other people to make us happy if we are not happy as individuals. It may be very difficult for us to love others if we do not love ourselves. All of us must be our own best friend and truly be on good terms with ourselves. Only after we feel genuinely good about ourselves, can we move out into the world and risk reaching out for relationships. This is the pattern that is essential for overcoming loneliness. It just does not happen; it is something we must strive for from day to day.

At no point do I maintain that this work is exhaustive, nor do I believe there is a recipe for a life devoid of loneliness. Because there are so many variables in human existence and because the variables interact in a very complicated manner, it is next to impossible to prescribe remedies for everyone. It is better to think, to feel, and then to examine one's pattern of life, in order to live, love, and grow.

Finally, I am looking at loneliness through the eyes of a man in his forties. I address my thoughts to all people, but especially to men. If I were writing on the subject of loneliness at the age of seventy, my thoughts might be very different from my present ones. Likewise, views on the lonely as seen by a forty-five-year-old woman might also be different from mine. And yet as human beings, I feel that we have more similarities than differences. Most of us have similar needs, and are searching for the best possible life as we see it.

two
Loneliness:
What We See
in Society

I will begin by making a bold statement. We are basically lonely people. Even though most of us spend many hours in some form of human interaction, we are close to only a few people. People cannot completely share their thoughts and feelings. As a result, they remain very much alone and often lonely. There may very well be a lot of truth in songs describing us as rocks and islands, but we are not born with lonely feelings. Something happens in our lives that leads to the emergence of these feelings. In other words, we create conditions for loneliness, as well as for happiness and fear. We, as human beings, are very much responsible for what and who we are.

I doubt if people today are very different from what they were forty years ago. However, the world has changed with a resulting influence on our life styles. Today all of us live under greater pressure; this is true for both adults and children. We demand more from ourselves as well as from those around us. We find that stress is one of the big problems in many areas of work. Individuals are leaving their jobs because they are unable to cope with the pressures. Whether the stress is the result of our own efforts or whether it comes from outside is not the problem. Stress is here to stay, and we must find ways of lessening its grip on our existence.

And yet I feel terribly excited about the present. Certainly I never experience the hardships my grandparents encountered. They were unable to enjoy the incredible inventions I take for granted. For example, I can fly across the country in four hours, whereas they needed that same length of time to visit friends a few miles away. I have twenty changes of clothing but they had only two. However, when the chips are down, I think they had a better time than I do. Some of the warmest feelings come to me when I reminisce about my childhood days when we went to town on Saturday night and dressed up on Sunday. I think there is a relationship between memories and loneliness.

Sometimes I feel very fortunate to have grown up in the 1940s, when life on a small farm was indeed very different from life in the city. I remember our little rural school with one teacher and thirty-eight children from grades one to ten. I used to walk to that building in thirty below zero weather to light the barrel-shaped stove; I was only eight years old but I was the school janitor. I often wonder what the teacher did without the teaching aids and projectors, principals, and counselors regularly found in today's schools. Life was so simple then. You laughed and cried; you worked hard and played hard. Sometimes life seemed to be suspended, and you wanted it to last for a long, long time. At times life was sad. I remember my best friend's mother dying, and how I could not imagine the same thing happening to me. Poor Peter was so afraid and lonely. I used to give him part of my bologna sandwich after school. Even then I knew I could not hug him or cry with him, since crying was something girls did quite often, but boys who cried were classed as sissies by their peers.

It is strange to think that I did not see a flush toilet until I was in grade ten, television came when I was at college, and I took my first plane ride when I started teaching. I look around me and see so many changes in the space of forty years. Here I sit in a comfortable house, with color television, and gadgets coming out of my ears. I often spend time pondering what I am going to wear to work or to the theater. How did I ever get by as a child with only two outfits? In those days you wore your clothes until they became threadbare.

What did I do on those long, cold January nights? There were no televisions, no records, no tapes, no library books, and no tickets to Hawaii. On the other hand, I knew where every student lived and I had been to each one's home. When I visited my friends, I was fed, no matter how plain or simple the food was. I remember one family had no butter and used to spread lard on their bread. At their house, I spread lard on my bread, but that was better than not having any bread.

My parents used to visit their friends frequently and we often had people at our house as well. I loved visiting friends with my father. In summer we used to travel in a buggy and in winter in a homemade, one-horse toboggan. The corners were great fun, because as the horse ran and turned, the toboggan used to slide out in a big semicircle. I used to lie under thick blankets and feel the cold wind in my face. I would look up and stare at the millions of stars in the black sky. I remember attending dances in our little school when everyone used to come to the socials. Children would dance around with the adults and then sprawl out on the benches and sleep. The coffee was made in a big tub, and the sandwiches were never very fancy. However, everyone laughed and talked and danced until the small hours of the morning. Life was not easy, but it was simple. People enjoyed one another and had many friends.

I am sure other people slip into thoughts of the past as well. The past does not appear bright for everyone but for me it holds many fond memories. Because of warmth and closeness that often appears absent today, life was basically not a lonely existence. The people in my environment felt good about themselves and there was a great deal of interdependency. People were not always in a hurry, and there always seemed to be enough time for a spur of the moment visit.

Today we are victims of our circumstances. We have been very carefully molded into "super" types. The media is partly responsible for this fine job, along with our own inadequacies and gullibilities. We just do not seem to have the good times we used to. We resist spontaneity but seem to thrive on structure and order. We are not fond of too many surprises, and tend to keep to ourselves.

Probably the reason why we cannot let go is because we are not totally certain who we really are. We do not have the self-confidence to be ourselves, and constantly worry how others see us. Again, the media does a beautiful job of creating a new world for us. It tells us what, where, and even *how* to do things. In other words, we are not even certain that we are able to think for ourselves.

So I look in the mirror and stare at my empty eyes. I mumble something to myself, turn around, and gaze out the window. It is no wonder that I feel lonely.

SOME HUMAN CHARACTERISTICS

But what about the present? I have lived in my house for nine years but have never even stood on a neighbor's doorstep, let alone gone into the house and eaten bread with lard. Sometimes I do not see people for weeks and even the children seem to play inside most of the time. The neighborhood people dash in and out of their driveways in their new cars. Because of automatic garage door openers, they are swallowed before I have a chance to see them from a distance. How can I talk to people if I never see them? I like to think that I am approachable and can carry on a conversation with most people, but human contact occurs far too infrequently. Unlike the old days, we seem to be quite independent and keep mainly to ourselves.

"Busyness" appears to be a key attribute of most people. There never seems to be time for them to slow down, to stretch out the hour, to take a slow walk, to stop and look closely at the flowers. We water and cultivate our roses but never seem to find the minutes to appreciate and savor their beauty. You see everyone dashing off to work and dashing off to play. They probably rush to the bathroom as well. It hardly seems possible that we once went to places more slowly, cooked more slowly and even talked more slowly. Why must we have "minute" rice, "instant" burgers and "instant" pudding? Why are people rushing off to church meetings, lodges, sororities and fraternities, meetings, clubs, and shopping trips? I cannot believe that everyone is such a good citizen or irreplaceable. I do believe this frantic activity is an indication of man's isolation. We seek refuge from loneliness in the cordiality of group activity. We are running away from something we fear. We have no one to blame but ourselves because we inflict regimentation on our lives. It appears as though this life style is here to stay.

What has happened to our values over the years? When I think of the 1940s and 1950s as compared to 1960–1980 not only have there been fantastic changes in technology but also in human values. A value is something an individual prizes or cherishes; it is highly personal. Unlike in the past, today many people like to impress others rather than themselves. They tend to be materialistic and to feel that what they buy has almost infinite meaning. They sometimes forget that money does not always solve basic problems. Some forget that they will not live forever and others simply forget.

There was a time when people were able to depend on one another. They valued each other and there was not as much superficiality. You were you, and people accepted you for what you were, rather than what you represented or pretended to be. Very often you could depend on a neighbor; there was time to stop and chat. There were no grand tours of houses, because once you stepped inside you pretty well saw the entire house. People dropped in because they could not phone beforehand. You ate the cake without the icing.

The incredible degree of mobility in our society is at least one factor contributing to the world of lonely people. I find it difficult to comprehend why thousands of people are moving to cities every month. This means that relationships are being weakened or eventually lost. Family and friends are often forgotten by men who seek a promotion or increase in salary. Long distance calls and letters will never take the place of eye contact or a hug. Rarely does separation make one feel closer.

I have lived in five different places and I find that over the years the few people I enjoyed seeing have gradually drifted away. When they come into the city, I hardly ever see them because I have commitments, or else they have their own plans. A brief, hurried phone call is simply not enough to maintain a genuine friendship.

Three years ago I spent four months in Tbilisi, USSR, working at the Uznadze Institute of Psychology. The wife of one of the professors was a very outgoing, lively individual. On the many occasions I visited their apartment, she would introduce me to her friends. She would add that some had been her friends since first grade. When I think of first or twelfth grade, or even college, I haven't the slightest clue as to where the people I once knew might be at this time. She mentioned that she has known some of her friends all her life. But unlike me, she has spent fifty years living in the same city, in the same neighborhood, and in the same apartment.

Today it appears that more and more people move to the cities to become cliff dwellers in the concrete canyons. Young people are seeking the good life portrayed by city slickers. After all, what action can one expect in a small town? Many young people feel there is more to do and see in the city. Quite often the search for happiness results in extreme loneliness. Disappointments and fear of taking risks can adversely affect an individual's morale. Sometimes the green grass around the old home appeals more to the individual than the black asphalt in the city.

The conglomeration of people in cities often provides an individual with little human contact. In your apartment you smell someone else's liver and onions, but you have little chance to see who eats it. It is rather strange. When you would like to see people, they never seem to be around. However, when you want some privacy and solitude, someone always seems to be hovering in the shadows. The timing never seems right.

The quest for solitude can sometimes result in strange paradoxes. Feeling tense and anxious, you may decide to leave your usual environemnt to seek the pleasures of the outdoors. Unfortunately, hundreds of others make the same decision. You get into your car and head for a camping area. After a lengthy search, with the sun burning you through the windshield, you spot a free table. No sooner do you unpack your bags of energy sustainers when a couple of dogs come around to sniff things over. You throw a stone at them but they turn around and bark at you. The people at the next table are having their second dozen beers and are quite oblivious to any noise, even their own. Isn't it funny how fresh air makes people happy? Finally you park your trailer. Bless the man who invented this "miracle-on-wheels" for those who seek privacy. As you emerge from your second home, you bump heads with another fellow who emerges from his car. After all, you must park so there is room for everyone. By ten o'clock, after a day of getting away from it all, you are ready to retire. However, the people ten feet across from you are just getting started. Isn't part of getting away from it all also living it up? By two A.M. you swallow two pills and succumb to complete exhaustion. On Sunday evening you are in a hurry to rest up for the next day's work. Traffic is very congested. Some fool passes you on the right. You swear. Ah, bless man and nature and all the joys they provide us. Many of you want privacy but also hate being alone. What would you do without others to lessen your loneliness? There seems to be a bit of irony here. We need people for companionship; but we frequently see them as getting in our way. We are not terribly overpopulated but our nerves are frazzled from day to day because of our encounters with others. The experience is almost enough to make us hate others, because we do not make exceptions and live by generalizations.

Even though we are not overpopulated, we see people as either slowing us down or thwarting our plans. All of us have experienced a long line at the supermarket express checkout counter. With plastic bags dangling from our hands, we sigh and shift our weight from one leg to the other. We patiently wait our turn. The line at a popular movie often stretches for two blocks; we contemplate our plans and decide to go home and make popcorn. We plan to attend a celebrity concert but when phoning for tickets, we are politely informed that everything was sold out four months ago. We curse without making a sound.

Thus we are faced with a serious dilemma. As human beings we should care for our fellow man, and yet we often see him as a nuisance. It is not surprising that individuals want to move away from the sprawling urban centers where people are so physically close, but emotionally distant. This is a serious matter that is becoming worse with every passing year. We need people and yet they often annoy and disappoint us.

The quest for position and power can lead to a rather lonely existence. The top of the pyramid is often cold and sterile. Business always comes first. Thinking competes with the incessant hum of the air conditioning system. Is it really worth it? Do power and money conquer all? I wonder what it is in some humans that makes them want power. I have known individuals who would almost give their life away so they could be at the top of the administrative heap.

How do they get there? They can make their way up by playing games, but often the gain is achieved by stepping on others as they climb the organizational structure. They must frequently use other people. They smile and shake hands when they truly do not feel like doing so. In this way they make a few enemies who see through them. They continue to fight and win, but the net result can lead to alienation and loneliness.

Power is very closely associated with status. But why is status so important in one's life? I recently heard a woman complain because her husband, who is an academic and administrator, had to make his own cement walk to his cabin. What is wrong with manual labor? What basic insecurity lurks in the minds of people who think they are important?

Along with power there is another situation which keeps people apart and thus minimizes the amount of interaction. This is the "problem" of success some people experience. These are the times when they discover who their true friends really are. Success often tends to create a great deal of uneasiness and jealousy on the part of others. How many times have people truly congratulated one another on some success or achievement? Why do many people secretly feel happy when they realize that others were not successful in their endeavors? How can one trust or be close to these people? Unfortunately, I find them in the majority. Colleagues, and even brothers and sisters, can be very jealous of each other's success in life. Successful people seldom seek the company of those who are jealous and self-centered.

A few months ago I won an all-expense-paid trip for two to New York City. I was terribly excited because I generally do not have much luck with contests. The experience was very interesting because of how individuals who knew me reacted towards me. I think two out of fifty people probably reacted in a happy, excited manner; however, the majority made no comment, or simply forced a smile when they saw me. People should be aware that loneliness and jealousy are very close friends.

Why is it so difficult for people to compliment others? Why can't they truly feel happy for you when you win a large sum of money? Why do you suddenly have a lot of "friends" who never seemed to care for you before? It is hardly any wonder that people do not trust each other and in fact, if they receive a compliment, they wonder what is going on. People tend to deny or play down any positive compliments. It is very difficult to give a compliment to another if you do not feel good about yourself as a person. On the other hand, if you feel confident and worthwhile, then you are able to reinforce and give of yourself to others.

Unfortunately, we still measure the worth of a man in terms of "whats," namely what he does, what he has, and what he is worth. We talk in terms of numbers. For example, he makes one million, has a two million dollar house with eleven bathrooms and four cars. There must be something sacred about being elite. We rarely think in terms of human sacrifice such as loneliness. We look at the incredible possessions but overlook the coldness that can accompany them. Why do so many of us aspire to such luxury? Why can't we be satisfied with who we are? Does success really lead to a better life? Is it possible to remember the red flowers in the window rather than the gold taps in the bathroom?

The inconsistency and pressures that man experiences are often accompanied by some form of withdrawal and often some degree of loneliness. For example, we want our children to be gentle and sensitive to the world around them; however, the more sensitive they are, the more hurt they can experience in their journey through life. Because adults often say one thing and do another, it is no wonder that children are confused with the double messages that they receive. We tell children not to cheat, yet we try every angle to cheat on tax forms. We see many fathers wanting their sons to be tough by engaging them in sports such as hockey or football. They feel it is necessary to portray some masculine image and the experience will be valuable in the future. I have seen sensitive children become emotionally devastated by this pressure. They are made to feel they are failures if they do not make the team. The children feel terribly rejected and as a result experience intense loneliness. How sad it is to see children suffering at such an early age because of parental desires. Problem children are usually a product of problem parents.

Affluence in our society has both positive and negative characteristics. We strive for the good life, but what do we do when we acheive it? Many of us are not aware when we have the good life because like unsatiated beasts, we are always looking for something better. For many, the rainbow shatters before the pot of gold is found.

I would be a fool to say that I like poverty more than affluence. My degree of affluence has enabled me to enjoy some aspects of life very much. I can wear what my heart desires, appreciate good music, good food, find leisure time and travel. But on the negative side, my affluence somehow makes me self-sufficient; it cuts me off from others, because in a sense I do not need others. Yes, I need other people's services, someone to phone an airline, to add my food bill, and to service my car, but the wealthier I become, the less I need other people to amuse me or to make my life more complete. There may be many Howard Hugheses leading moldy lives in utter privacy.

The more isolation you crave, the more affluence you need. Why bother looking at cars, when people will drive them to your house for examination. You wouldn't dream of going to a public pool when you have your own. You can have a meal catered in your own house, or fly to Paris for lunch, and get away from people who might ordinarily watch you eat a tuna sandwich. Your entire world can be at your fingertips. Even though not all affluent people lead sad, miserable lives, affluence may lead to isolation and the silent company.

Rich or poor, all of us have the same end. Many of us fear death, and yet the actual fear is really a part of us and of our loneliness. Of course we do not constantly dwell on something so remote and frightening as death. It must be the loneliest experience in this universe. Even though we are very well acquainted with the silent company, I cannot even begin to imagine the magnitude of loneliness associated with death. Even the thought of it makes me realize how important it is to enjoy each sunrise, each smile, and each moment.

SOME HUMAN INSTITUTIONS

Whether the family in our society is disintegrating or lacking the cohesiveness it had in the past, the extended family appears to be nonexistent today. Our modern society has devised special segregated structures for our old people. An immediate relative hardly ever has any desire to look after an elderly parent. I feel that one tragic aspect of our society is the lack of respect for the aged. Retired pensioners must be among the loneliest people on this earth.

A woman I know who is a volunteer for the "Meals-on-Wheels" program often talks about some of the old people she sees. In one case, a man lives in a small room up three flights of stairs. He walks with difficulty. His room is practically devoid of furniture and he uses his cupboard top for a table. However, he does have a large color photograph of his son's family. The photograph stares him in the face as he eats his meals. Why should an old man lead such a harsh existence, if his relatives are alive and well? Why is it not possible to have the old person live with the family? We often hear a person say, "Well, you don't know my mother. We never see eye to eye. After one hour we fight like dogs. I wouldn't want her around me all the time, because she would drive me crazy!" I hope this is an exception rather than a rule. My grandmother lived with my mother for forty years. Some of my fondest memories of childhood are the hours I spent with my grandmother. She not only helped with the farm chores, but she found time to tell me a few fairy tales, to walk among the trees, and to listen to the crunch of snow under our feet. I regard her as one of the most fantastic persons I have ever known. Moreover, I never recall my mother arguing or fighting with her.She felt important, she was needed and we loved her. I do not think she ever felt lonely.

Many other people feel they would be happier on their own. They feel they are a burden on the younger people and interfere with their life style. This cannot be a natural feeling; they have probably sensed the message from some members of the family or they have heeded the advice of their friends. On the other hand, there is no reason why a person should not live on his own if he is perfectly content with this life style. Certainly there is nothing negative about such a decision any more than a young person wanting to be on his own.

I feel that grandchildren and grandparents are the ones who usually suffer in the typical family structure. There is no one who can truly pamper, accept, and love a grandchild as a grandparent can. The grandparent does not have the responsibilities for the grandchild as he did for his own children. There is no pressure to act in any way but a natural one. I realize at this point in my life that many potentially lonely days during my childhood were alleviated because of the happiness provided by grandparents.

A perfect embodiment of loneliness in our society is mass socialization, as for example, the typical cocktail party. I love to make fun of this Western institution. I have vowed that the only way one could get me to the next cocktail hour would be to drug me or drop me down through the roof. The most superficial hours of my life have been spent at these empty gatherings. Never again will I put myself in a position where a person pretends to converse with me as he simultaneously scans the crowd to see if there is anyone more important around. I hate the experience of having a person wave to another over my head, expecially if he is getting my undivided attention. The situation is fairly typical. The social gathering is a brief escape into a world of gowns, ties, forced smiles, and "renewed" friendships. More often than not, the motive is to make an appearance because it is the appropriate thing to do. Often it is a meeting of the "right people" with limp handshakes. I wonder if more men than women enjoy cocktail parties. From my own experience, men usually tag long because the women want them to go. Why do people go to parties because they feel they *have* to go?

Mind you, dinner parties are not always much better. Some food, wine, and a gathering of close friends create genuinely stimulating experience. However, a crowded "stand and spill" feast may cause heartburn and indigestion. Why do you go? You only have an obligation to pay them back. I know one person who has been in a circle of dinner parties almost every weekend, as he has been unsuccessfully trying to obtain several administrative positions. Why does he do it? There are times when he may need support while seeking some post; his "friends" give him their votes when they think of his fantastic oyster soup. By the way, the person I am referring to is also a very lonely man.

I could go on and on describing our forms of entertainment and how they reflect our lives. However, the point I wish to make is that mass socialization is probably here to stay. There are reasons for this. Many of us feel safer and less vulnerable in crowds. You can behave in a manner that would not be acceptable on a one-to-one basis. It is one way of showing emotions without too much risk involved. It is useful to let off steam and it appears to be easier to do in large groups. It gives one a chance to observe others and to learn.

Mass socialization as a form of entertainment is a reflection of our busy times. Because we know many people, it seems reasonable to invite them all at once and get the entertaining over with. Quite often we invite people because they invited us in the past. Entertainment soon becomes a vicious circle of paying people back. I would rather eat hamburger with someone I truly enjoy than steak with someone who is merely paying me back. But food was never very high on my list of priorities.

Why do people participate in forms of large group entertainment? Our society is not an easy place for meeting people. Any person seeking a relationship might think there are more possibilities in a group function. We are aware that there have been successful relationships which began with a group introduction. The common feeling is that since there is little to lose, it is worth taking a chance.

But even though there is a chance to renew old acquaintanceships or meet new people, I cannot regard large scale socializing as an effective tool against loneliness. For the minority of winners there is a majority of losers. The important idea is not to fool ourselves about having a good time and to be deluded by fantasy and hope. Often the net result is only wasted time.

Another Western institution that tears at the hearts of lonely people, especially those in their twenties, is Saturday night! The standard belief is that this is a time for fun, joy, and all that goes with it. To stay home is to admit defeat. What a feeling to go to bed at ten with only the radio for company, while other people your age are at the fun spots. How awful you might feel without a date. You phone someone and ask if they will accompany you to a movie. Even if you come home at ten, you feel at ease with yourself; it was Saturday night and you were out. No, it is not the night for lonely people. However, there is nothing sacred about Saturday night or any other night for that matter. There is no reason to think of yourself as a winner or a loser if you stay home. Have you recently experienced an evening enjoying your quiet moments reading, listening to music, or just relaxing? Of course it is great to share these experiences with someone close to you, but sometimes there is peace and contentment in being by oneself. Remember, not everybody out there is having the time of their lives; many people are crying.

How can we forget to mention Christmas? There is no other holiday that can so tear at the lonely, vulnerable hearts of many people and turn potential joy to sadness. Music and spoken words remind us that it is a season for joy and good will. It is a time for friends and family to join in happy communication. But what about the people who have neither family nor friends? Christmas sends shivers down the spines of many who worry about plans for the festive season. It is not a time to be alone; it is not a time for the lonely.

Does Christmas have its intended meaning for the majority of people? For many of us it is a time to rush around shopping malls, partying and exchanging pleasantries. We stay up late and tire easily. We attend staff parties that permit us to have fun as only adults can. We wake in the morning with splitting headaches and even silence pierces our senses. We swear our head and body are in separate places. Let's face it. Holidays are for us to enjoy in whatever manner we find desirable. They are a brief respite from the workaday world. Christmas may be commercialized, and it may be devoid of its religious meaning, but like millions of others, I think it's great.

But what about the people who are truly alone and surrounded by a world of sadness? What about the person who walks to the pizza parlor and returns home to an empty room on Christmas Eve? For many it is a time for travel, laughter, or a truly holy night, but for others it is a lonely, silent night.

In our society, loneliness thrives in singles bars, lonely hearts clubs, and massage parlors. Even though the three do not fulfull the same purpose for any one individual, a certain type of companionship is usually sought. Most people who frequent these places hope to alleviate their loneliness.

What happens in many bars? You move from the tensions of day to the tensions of night. You reach for your drink as your eyes survey the smoke-filled room. Will you be lucky tonight? Will you be going home alone to a lonely room in the lonely night? The truth of the matter is that bars are often a place for one-night stands or sporadic meetings. I cannot imagine that there are many long-lasting relationships that develop at such places. However, the surprise is often a good escape. A person thinks they have very little to lose, and the net result can be a laugh or a cry.

The lonely hearts clubs are very much in the same category as bars. Usually one associates them with the separated, the divorced, and the widowed. The advertisements are often very promising. For a few dollars, you can begin a new and exciting existence. The sponsors always end up as winners; they have your money before you begin your excitement. What do you have to lose? You must possess the courage to risk when you are in the company of other people who are looking and searching for mates. If you do not feel self-confident, you may experience rejection and be hurt by others at these institutions. But one never really knows. There is always the possibility of finding the right person at the right time.

The typical city newspaper carries ads for a number of massage parlors found in and around the town. The ads emphasize service from beautiful girls, and of course, the gentle touch. It may be better to be touched by a stranger than not to be touched at all. For the lonely person in a lonely city, the money may be well spent. After all, some people would agree that spending time with a lively, willing person is certainly more worthwhile than sitting alone in front of a television set. This is a question of priorities.

I do not want to downgrade the purpose of this type of institution. Once in a while, you read about the parlors being raided by police because they go beyond their function. Is this good or bad? I cannot answer this. For some people, the thought in itself can be somewhat revolting; for others, it may cause laughter. I do not feel that moral issues are relevant to the questions I am asking regarding forms of entertainment. However, there are many lonely people who will do almost anything to avoid the pain of the silent company.

SOME HUMAN TOOLS

We live in a world of commercialism, a world of invention that staggers the mind. Man has invented many tools to make his life more pleasant and easier to cope with. Only when I return home after spending a few months in some remote part of the world do I truly realize how we take for granted all of our fantastic inventions.

I still find some aspects of modern living unbelievable. How incredible to be in Europe in a matter of hours. How efficient to be able to dial several numbers and hear the phone ring four thousand miles away. I cannot believe my eyes when I can watch, via satellite, what happened in France only a few hours ago. I can even warm up a piece of pie at the snap of a finger. There is no end to what money can buy. And yet, as strange as it may seem, some of the inventions also help to keep us apart, and to make us feel inadequate as human beings. Somehow I feel that I am only a number in a huge conglomerate. If I disappeared from the face of this earth, I would be missed by only a small number of people. But what would happen if all the light bulbs disappeared, not to mention our television sets or even screwdrivers? Even though some of our tools appear to lessen the tensions of loneliness, they also do their share to diminish self-worth, and the quality of human relationships.

One aspect of our lives that does not stop loneliness is the media and all the commercialism that it entails. As informative as television may be on some occasions, I cannot imagine a person spending up to six hours at a time in front of the set. Mind you, I have heard of some people turning on their televisions set just for the noise it produces. They somehow feel that silence is just too deadly for the soul, that it is the brother of loneliness. There is one positive factor to consider. Your superficial company can be turned on or off at will. This may not be too easily accomplished with people.

Television does not encourage any interaction among individuals. If one person likes to watch soap operas, and the other hates them, one will have to withdraw to another room. How can one communicate anything exciting to an individual when he is slouched in a chair with his eyes glued to the set during the third down? Conversation is an interesting phenomenon; people need to be in the right frame of mind to converse, and timing may or may not correspond to this mood. In other words, a lot of our communication must be spontaneous and natural. It is difficult to put aside one hour for sharing ideas and for actually listening. Children are especially spontaneous in their conversation. When they arrive from school, they want to tell you immediately what happened during the day.

You do not encourage their spontaneity if you tell them you are busy and there is no time to listen to their stories. They want to tell you now and not after dinner. We can learn a great deal from children; we can learn all over agian.

However, television can be an escape from loneliness. It can provide a few hours of entertainment that takes your mind off reality. There are times when a person may watch special programs for five or six hours consecutively, but this is highly unlikely to occur day after day. Television, like movies, is a great escape from the harshness of this world.

One other aspect of television needs some comment, namely the constant barrage of advertisements that face us. Oddly enough, some people would think that these countless messages have very little to do with everyday existence. This is far from the case. Someone tells us what to drink, what to wear, what to drive, what perfumes are sexy, what to use for shiny teeth and hair, and on and on. We may cry our hearts out, but we will probably never look like the woman running in slow motion through a field of daisies, with her hair sparkling in the sun. Clothing does not look quite as good on us either. Our hair looks a bit greasy and we think our noses are a little large. Why can't we look like the man who is on the cover of *Esquire?* The overall result of advertising can make us feel inadequate, and as a result we do not feel as good about ourselves as we should. This is crucial in the world of loneliness, because to avoid that hollow feeling it is necessary to feel good about ourselves, to look at our positive characteristics, without dwelling on our negative points. Advertising does not help in this area.

Even though what I am saying may sound somewhat absurd, proof of the effect advertising has on people can be determined by the amount of money they spend purchasing goods. Some people think that having a big new car creates instant happiness. It may provide a false type of security that some people badly need. Their problem is more closely related to themselves. Positive feelings of self-worth are necessary. If we are certain that a new car will help us feel good about ourselves, then by all means, the car should be purchased. We are often led to believe that what is good for others is good for us. It is of great benefit to reexamine our values from time to time. The result can lead to more self-acceptance and thus to fewer lonely times in our lives.

The wonderful invention of the telephone has had an incredible effect upon our lives. I cannot think of any other invention that can make us run in the middle of night, run out of the bathroom, or run in the middle of a burning meal. We can ignore a person who is attempting to communicate with us but we find it difficult to ignore the ring of a telephone. How many lonely hours have we spent waiting for a phone call? How many times have we seen long distance helping to reunite happy families? How many times have we made a call because we were lonely at the time?

Telephones are a wonderful tool we must agree. However, for some individuals they may be just another way of expressing their loneliness. Why is it necessary to spend one or two hours on the phone at one time? Is it not to lessen some of your internal tensions? Do you really think that the other person is interested in listening to you as they shift the receiver from ear to ear? Is it not easier to phone than to meet a person face-to-face where you might use some eye contact or show some nonverbal cues while you converse? The situation is no different from the incessant talker at the cocktail party. Beneath all the chatter there is probably a person who is very much alone and lonely.

Today most people feel that money is one of the most important commodities in their lives. Somehow, everyone has to work because there is so much to buy; so much is available. Every day the paper is filled with pages of super buys, everything from better washers and faster boats to greener grass and more exotic cosmetics. But all of it costs money! If you cannot pay for it now, you can pay later. We still have not realized that money does not buy relationships and money does not act as a barrier against loneliness. Your mink coat, plush carpet, and Cadillac do not necessarily make you a happier person. In fact, as we chase after the dollar we leave a lot of our values behind. We will do almost anything to gain a few bucks. If we spend the hours in constructive work instead of negotiating for more money, we would at least start in the right direction. Do not misunderstand me. Money is important; it gives us freedom. I can think of the trek I would like to take in Nepal if I had the spare cash.

We should view money in terms of what it can do for us rather than as an end in itself. For many, the dollar rules with a tight, greedy grasp.

I think that very few people spend time by themselves or in solitude to contemplate what life is all about. How many of you get up, have your coffee, rush off to work, then complain about what you are doing? After work you rush home to cope with everyday chores. Chances are that you rush off again, or you retire for the evening with a book or in front of the television. Do you question if it is worth it? I am amazed that the majority of people dislike their work and they strive only for the dollar. It is no wonder that loneliness finds many victims.

Life is a series of steps. What was important when you were twenty may not be as important when you are thirty. You learn by living and growing. You reach a point where life is perfect, and you could go on forever. Then the bottom falls out. After the fall, you pick yourself up and begin the climb again. This can be a very lonely time. This is a time when you use most of your strength just to survive. When you do make it, you are a greater person. You have changed, you have grown, and you have learned. Money cannot buy this experience.

There is one other aspect of money that is worth mentioning. It is an excellent way to split families apart. Constant energy is spent on fighting over property and money. Parents and grandparents would have burnt the stuff if they knew what was going on among the surviving "loved" ones. I know of a brother and sister who refuse to look at each other because one was willed five or six thousand dollars. I have seen a happy family completely destroyed when one spouse inherited a large sum of money. There was so much debate over what to do with it, where to invest it, what to buy with it, that they had little time for each other. Soon after, the relationship disintegrated and each individual began to experience intense loneliness. A large diamond can reflect the gloom in a woman's eyes. The new overcoat does not always feel softer than the old one. We have reached a point where a man is not judged for his ability but for the size of his bank account. Money does not always reflect the value of a man or his accomplishments. Man should be judged in terms of his human qualities.

SOME THOUGHTS
ON THE FUTURE

In addition to all the materialism and mass socialization that dominate our society, we are living in an age of uncertainty. Regardless of what we experienced in the past and what we think of the present, the thought of what future years have in store leads me to sigh, not out of boredom but out of fear and apprehension.

History is never at a standstill and I have heard that it does repeat itself, but I am in no mood for surprises. I have experienced real war, cold war, and no war. But today, I worry more about my safety, my security as well as what is in store for my children. I have to cope with incredible pressures and there are days when I can only think about my own survival.

Let me be more specific. My dollar used to buy much more than it does today. I really do not think it is too wise to save excessively, because in five years it will likely be worth much less than it is today. My income does not increase very much, and yet it seems that each year I must give up more and more of my earnings. There are always a number of payments staring me in the face. The overall feeling is reflected by the hollowness beneath my rib cage.

Furthermore, there is no great amount of security in terms of work. Somehow permanence has lost its meaning. Even buildings that are around can be torn down in a matter of minutes. I am never really certain that I can maintain my present position for the next ten or twenty years. Even the thought of being idle sends shivers down my spine. I have great sympathy for the unemployed.

Man's inhumanity to man never ceases to amaze me. I know what the atomic bomb can do but I understand the neutron bomb is even more efficient. Nations continue to buy more and more armaments. The Middle East resembles a volcano. Day-to-day events affect me, if not directly, at least in an emotional way. Nations are constantly in verbal battle. I am told that baby seals are being clubbed to death. I also know that a lot of resources that I took for granted will not be around forever. Maybe when I grow old, I will be looking at pictures of what a forest really looked like.

What does all of this do to me? I become apprehensive, I really wonder if all the struggle is worth the effort. I spend many moments in thought. Some people I knew well have died of heart attacks. Some committed suicide. I must cope with the pressures. Furthermore, I must trust my fellow man and establish relationships which are necessary for my survival. I must think in a positive vein as often as I possibly can. My self-image cannot afford to falter. I need every part of it to survive in this human jungle. I must continue to live in the present, but keep one eye on the future. I must continue to examine my life space in terms of self and needs, for loneliness is never far away.

three
Loneliness:
How Needs Are Related
to Feelings

No two human beings have the same physical, physiological, or emotional characteristics. However, all of us have certain basic needs which are similar regardless of who or where we are. For example, to some degree all of us require food, affection, and approval from others.

Needs are related to loneliness. When some of our needs are not satisfied, we tend to react accordingly. The reaction often corresponds to the degree of need deprivation. We usually act out our feelings in some way or we withdraw into our own little worlds. Either way, we are bound to experience some loneliness. If I give and receive no affection, I feel insecure and receive no positive feedback from significant people around me. My feelings are affected. I find I do not feel great and my self-esteem drops to a low level. More and more I become a victim of loneliness. At the same time, I have difficulty in relating to other people and establishing close meaningful relationships; I seem to be on the defensive most of the time. I again become a victim of loneliness.

If we are one of the few fortunate people who have our basic needs satisfied, then we are able to sit on top of the human pyramid. We can feel somewhat special because we have left loneliness behind us. Our perceptions are uncluttered and we can see almost forever. Many of us have the potential to become one of these fortunate individuals. We need honest awareness and a desire to grow, to strive toward being someone we thought was not within our grasp. We do have a choice. We can spend our energy spinning our wheels in one place, or we can devote our time and energy to moving ahead and leaving mere existence in the dust.

An entire book could be written to explain the functions and importance of human needs. There is no denying that needs are important factors in our behavior. The difficulty is to identify some of them and note how they relate to feelings of loneliness, which can emerge because of an unfulfilled need.

Everyone has similar needs. Human beings require food, air, water, a certain amount of security, and some affection. The degree to which our needs must be satisfied in order to function is a highly individual matter. Just as some people eat more than others, some require more affection than others. But there are important factors that one must consider in the realm of needs. To take affection as an example, the quality of the affection given as well as the source of the affection are very important variables to be considered. Some people have a great need to be among crowds all the time, whereas others are content to be alone in an isolated environment most of their lives and honestly feel satisfied with their existence. I prefer to look at people's needs in general rather than examine the needs of isolated cases. Often the needs are not that different; only the amount and quality differ.

Some people emphasize the needs relating to action, meaning that we are energetic creatures requiring a fair amount of activity for our existence. Others emphasize the importance of autonomy. Even though an individual fits into a certain group, he must have the ability to disagree and give reasons for his disagreement. I have heard visitors from foreign countries make comments about our methods of raising children. They feel that we tend to teach autonomy at an early age. Children are often encouraged to make decisions which are beyond their reasoning ability. I recall one father asking his four-year-old what he thought was the right car for their family. Children are literally forced into high chairs so they can learn to feed themselves. I have seen mothers in some societies feed their five-year-old children. Some psychologists comment on the pressures children experience, not only from their peers, but from adults as well. Growing up is no simple task!

When we inquire what keeps us going, I immediately think of *Toward a Psychology of Being* by Abraham Maslow. His discussion of human needs seems very adequate for our discussion here, and especially appropriate to the concept of loneliness. This does not mean that there are other views of needs that are not important, but the ideas of Maslow are relevant to each of us. The needs he describes are structured somewhat like a pyramid. The first needs are very basic and general to us all. Before we attempt to fulfull the higher needs, those in the lower hierarchy must be satisfied. We are always seeking to satisfy some need. If we cannot satisfy one level of needs, it is next to impossible to move up to the next level.

Furthermore, we must think in terms of the whole person, the total me or you. We think of the whole person as being motivated, which in turn affects his behavior. For example, when a man is thirsty, his energy is directed twoard a search for water, and nothing else matters. In addition, I think it is difficult to isolate needs and study them individually. Man is a very complex individual, and when we look at a need such as love, we appreciate its complexity as well as its interrelationships with other needs. Let us examine some of these needs and discuss their importance.

PHYSICAL NEEDS

The most basic, powerful, and obvious need that all humans require is the need for physical survival, and includes liquid, food, oxygen, sleep, shelter. These needs are necessary for the survival of man. However, there may be some substitution. For example, hunger may be partially satisfied by drinking water or even smoking a cigarette. Also, these physiological needs are the most prepotent of all needs. A person who is lacking food has no great desire for love, safety, or even self-esteen.

Let us look more closely at the need to satisfy hunger. Most of us are not familiar with the deprivation in this area. If your stomach feels hunger pangs, you seek a grocery store or refrigerator. As a matter of fact, when you look around, you get the feeling that most people spend more time satisfying this need than some of the others.

Starvation must be a terribly lonely experience. I cannot describe it personally, but I have seen living examples of starving people. My father often recalls the problems he and his parents experienced after they returned to their village near Brest, Poland. (They had avoided the horrors of World War I by fleeing to the central part of Russia.) His mother gathered weeds, boiled them and fed the family. I remember some of the faces I saw in Peru and Guatemala; these are etched in my memory forever. I remember an old, wrinkled woman, almost immobile with pleading eyes, too weak to speak, begging for food. The rusty tin can which she feebly held told the whole story. I remember a group of children about six years of age waiting around while I was having some lunch. After I finished they quickly gathered the chicken bones and leftover bits of bread into a bag. Tears flooded my eyes.

When a person is hungry, his capacities are directed to satisfy this need. Intelligence, memory, and habits are simply tools to gratify hunger. Any individual abilities which cannot be used to obtain food are left to lie dormant. The desire to sing a love song, to buy new shoes, to study science, or to buy a new record are forgotten or deemed of little importance. No other interest exists for the man who is dangerously hungry. He thinks about food, he dreams about food, he perceives only food, and he wants only food.

When an individual is dominated by a certain need, his whole attitude toward the future tends to change. His philosophy tends to be very closely related to the need deficit. For the man who is extremely hungry, his Utopia is a place with an abundance of food. He thinks that if he can have food for the rest of his life, he will be the most satisfied person on earth. He will never want anything more, because his life is defined in terms of food and eating. Even the thought of other needs is brushed aside as irrelevant. Mention the need for love, or freedon, or even a philosphy of life, and the hungry person will ignore you. He would say that they do not fill his empty stomach. We can appreciate the powerful influence that food has on one's life. Although I am speaking of hunger here, I can elaborate in much the same way on other physiological needs. It is true that all people do not have the same level of needs, even that of food. I know of a person who once sat down and ate an entire ham. He literally licked the bone clean. He is a sprawling mass of fat. For him, eating and drinking constitute life.

Man is a creature of wants, who throughout life is always desiring something. He rarely reaches a stage in life where he has complete satisfaction, and if he does, it lasts for only a short time. Basically, when one desire is satisfied, it is only a matter of time before there are other desires to be fulfilled. Taking our example of hunger, it is also true that man lives not by bread alone, when there is bread. When man's stomach is in good shape, other needs emerge that tend to dominate his behavior. When these needs in turn are satisfied, more complex needs will emerge.

Climbing the ladder of needs continues throughout man's existence. Once a want is satisfied it is no longer a want. However, it does not mean that the want will not emerge again when it is thwarted in the future. The behavior of man is very much determined by his unsatisfied needs. Actually, when we speak of hunger we are really speaking of appetites, since most of us have not experienced true hunger. One interesting note might be added to the discussion. If an individual has always had a certain need satisfied, he is usually better equipped to tolerate the deprivation of that need sometime in the future.

THE NEED FOR SECURITY

Once the physiological needs are satisfied, a new set emerges which Maslow describes as the safety needs. These needs usually include protection, freedom from fear, stability, security, the need for structure, order, and law. If the physiological needs are satisfied, it is quite possible for an individual to organize his behavior toward the search for safety. Again, his dominant goal influences his world outlook, as well as his values and basic philosphy. If the situation is extreme, a man in this state may live for safety alone.

Although safety needs are generally satisfied in the normal, healthy adult, this may not be the case for infants, children, or neurotic adults. For example, infants will react globally when they are disturbed, startled, or handled roughly: for example, when they sense a loss of support in their mother's arms. Quite often they also experience colic, vomiting, or sharp pains. The infant experiences instability instead of stability, and his environment becomes a place of uncertainty.

Parents may be interested to know about another aspect of their child's need for safety. A child prefers some type of routine which has no disruption. He wants an environment which is predictable and orderly. If he experiences degrees of injustice, unfairness, or inconsistency, the child may become anxious, and see the world as a place which is unpredictable, unsafe, and unreliable. Children thrive in a system which has a schedule of some kind, a system with at least some rigidity and some type of routine. Children need limits, and these are necessary not only in the present but in the future as well.

Children do not always thrive in complete permissiveness. The topic of discipline has come up for discussion in many homes and schools. Discipline is very necessary because it designates caring for the child. It means setting some type of limit, some type of order which hopefully mirrors the world. Quite often a parent or teacher does not discipline because he fears rejection or loss of the child's love. The rejection is accompanied by a sense of anxiety and failure on the adult's part. A child may seek attention from other sources, and in the process defy the parent. The net result is an aching heart, sadness, and a feeling of loneliness. By the way, I am not advocating a tyrannical approach where you abuse the child verbally or physically. I am advocating firmness and fairness so that the child can operate within some defined framework. This is necessary for the child's survival in this world.

I have seen examples where limits have not been set, and my basic reaction was disgust, not toward the child but toward the parent. The other day, one of my neighbor's daughters, who is sixteen, was driven home from school by a student friend. After hugging and kissing inside the car, they emerged and continued in front of the house. Obviously I do not look for such situations but I happened to be cutting the grass on the front lawn. Four eight-year-olds were skipping a few feet away. Feeling somewhat embarrassed, they moved into a garage.

This freedom, this lack of concern, this insensitiveness toward children often sets the groundwork for many unhappy children. Children who are becoming very isolated and also very lonely begin to seek some company that will allow them to escape from an intolerable situation. We read about the thousands of children who run away from home every year. We read about the large number of teenage girls who are spotted by pimps and led into a life of prostitution. These are not happy children! How sad to think that they should be at home playing with their dolls and reading children's books. We also read about the incredible suicide rate among adolescents. The seeds of discontent are sown early in the home. Children experience incredible loneliness, and instead of coping with the world, they escape and lose themselves. Often it is a one-way street. Many of these children are beautiful people who, like flowers, never enjoyed the proper environment in which their beautiful colors could develop. Instead, they slowly wither away to nothing.

Let me again emphasize that the typical child wants an orderly, safe, organized, predictable world that he can depend on. He does not want a world of surprise, with unexpected and general chaos. He wants someone who can be his protector; he wants a shield from harm.

The healthy adult in our society is generally sufficiently protected so that most of his safety needs are satisfied. In general, we have sufficient political stability, orderliness, and peace to enable us to operate at a higher level of needs. Safety needs, unlike hunger needs, do not entirely motivate and organize our total behavior.

However, safety is not absolute in our society. We are constantly hearing or reading about rape, murder, and extortion. Even in smaller cities, there are often cases of shooting, hostage dramas, and physical abuse. My father's uncle lived in Brooklyn for forty years but had to move because of his safety needs. There were times when he could not go for a walk without a group of muggers approaching him with knives and demanding money. On many occasions a female will not venture onto the street after hours because of the dangers that may be lurking. The security in some of our penal institutions is unbelievable. We find closed circuit television, locks, chains and bars, security men, dogs, high fences, and everything short of hidden missiles. The situation does not appear to be getting better. I live in a very quiet neighborhood, and after a recent trip, I returned home to find my stereo components and television set missing. I was stunned. I could not believe that some thieves broke into my house during my absence. I became very conscious of my safety needs, and went to the local hardware store to purchase more locks.

The barricades we build around us do not facilitate closer interaction. There is a basic mistrust among humans, and the first thought that comes to mind is caution. Even though we may give another the benefit of the doubt, there are too many unpleasant experiences that can occur if we are totally unprepared. Our basic mistrust of each other and the levels of fear that people exhibit toward each other do nothing to alleviate loneliness.

Society reacts to safety needs, especially when there are threats to forms of law and order. If there is any threat of chaos, society can regress from higher needs to the world of safety needs. One can imagine the havoc played on man by war, when needs come tumbling down to the level of basic survival. Also one can better understand why there is acceptance of military rule or dictatorship in some of our societies. This does not mean that military rule is the answer, but people cannot function where there is chaos. We thrive and grow when security surrounds us.

One other aspect of security prevalent in our society bears mentioning. Today people feel quite insecure in their work and thus in their ability to earn money. The dollar is still interpreted as a form of security. As money loses its value, people who have saved for their future become fearful when their budget does not cover what they had planned. Many elderly citizens feel the current economic pinch. Because of layoffs and unemployment, people do not have the security they need for everyday living. Today people are not certain if they will be able to keep their same, comfortable jobs all their lives. In order to hold onto their jobs, many individuals who are not totally self-confident and secure resort to company politics to maintain their positions. They say the right things to the right people at the right time in order to survive. Some must wonder if the game is worth all the effort. They must be terribly lonely people in their little worlds. Loneliness thrives in an insecure world.

Furthermore, some people seem to survive in the world of lonely work. It is interesting to know that a few individuals will put themselves in positions that have doors closed to security. Often the type of work they do molds them more and more into very lonely souls. People who walk a tightrope must suffer hours of tension and turmoil from day to day. Executive positions in companies, some government positions, and some types of negotiations work probably fall into this category. Some people will sacrifice their psychological welfare for positions of power, prestige, and money. Many of these poor souls are not necessarily secure, happy people; for some, life must be a lonely nightmare.

THE NEED FOR LOVE

If there are various degrees of loneliness because of physiological and security needs deficits, the apex of loneliness is reached when there is lack of affection among individuals. It is my belief that love for self and others is one of the most important human needs. It is one of the best agents for keeping the silent company at bay.

Recently a friend mentioned that she had a contribution to my discussion on loneliness. On a washroom wall she saw some writing that stood out from all the graffiti. The individual wrote that if she were not lonely she would not be writing on the washroom wall. The statement was followed by a poem dedicated to love. It is not possible for everyone to admit to loneliness and to the need for love. The anonymous writer was able to express her feelings; she must be congratulated for having this ability. If we agree that affection is important for all of us, then we should examine the need in greater detail.

If physiological and safety needs are satisfied, then we see the emergence of needs for love, affection, and belonging. I might add that when the former two needs are not satisfied, man tends to react with anger and fear. Man feels that society owes him a living, at least some basic form of living that humans need for survival. On the other hand, if love and belonging as well as other higher needs are not fulfilled, man tends to react not with anger but with feelings of frustration. The amount of frustration one feels would probably reflect the degree of need deprivation. Do people around us exhibit signs of frustration? I think that it is all too common.

What appears to be the immediate effect on a person when he is deprived of love? Loneliness, intense loneliness, and a sense of despair. Loneliness is accompanied by feelings of failure and rejection, both very unpleasant feelings to be experienced by anyone. Rejection by family, friend, or spouse is one of the most traumatic jolts that a psychological system has to cope with. The feelings of rejection, loneliness, and depression may be the pattern for any individual experiencing some of life's traumas involving the loss of love.

However, some adults who hide their feelings never cry over the loss of love. They can rationalize that they did not lose much and there are many other affairs to be had. If they are rejected, they do not ponder their situation, or feel the resultant hurt. When they experience a moment of loneliness, they dial someone who is available, as if they were buying a spare part to a machine. If company is not available, there is always a cigarette and a Scotch on the rocks to soothe the nerves. How wonderful that nature has means of looking after us!

I frequently refer to children because so many are natural, honest, and beautiful. Probably some parents and teachers would not agree with me, but associating with this young generation can be a very fulfilling experience. I remember visiting an elementary school. The first grade students were coming down the stairs, and even though they did not know who I was, three of them came to me with their drawings. While I was looking at their work, they put their arms around my legs. I patted them on their heads and remarked how cute they were. Soon there was a crowd around me. They all seemed to want some affection and attention.

Look at our children. Our lonely, fragile children who cannot think as "deeply" as we can, who cannot dial-a-date, and who hopefully, do not pour themselves a Scotch. "It's a tough life to be a kid these days," I heard one adult say. "So much to put up with. Mind you, it's also tough being a parent. It's a tough world period!"

If we can remember only one thing, it should be that all children require love. They require genuine affection, not hours of it, but moments of true affection. One minute of a "warm hug" and "I love you more than anybody", enables a child to grow. This one minute cannot be replaced by five chocolate bars, six new dresses, or a new stereo set. To give affection seems so easy, and yet in reality is so difficult to do. How difficult it is for a father to hug his teenage daughter and ruffle her hair. How easy it is to say "No, you're not going and that is that. I don't want to hear another word about it, okay?" The feeling the child gets from being loved and wanted is the greatest feeling he can have. It provides a foundation as solid as concrete, because it gives him a chance to stand tall and to grow. To love a child and to make him feel good about himself is as important as birth itself.

What fun it is to be a parent when you love the role. The same holds true for teachers or other adults who work with children. A good teacher is one who nurtures the child with knowledge and with care. He must like children, want to be with them, and make the children glad to be with him as well. To be a parent, teacher, or a counsellor and simply go through the motions is not enough. One must give more than knowledge; one must give of oneself.

There is one basic problem with love and affection. How can we give to our children, to other children, to adults, or to anyone when we do not receive? This is not quite the same as gift giving, but much more intense and involved. In other words, if an individual has been loved as a child and has grown up with this necessary need fulfilled, there is a high probability that this person will grow into an adult who can freely give his warmth and affection. During our lifetime, we can consciously attempt to change and not model ourselves after poor parental behavior. However, we find that the father who beats his child is often one who was himself beaten by his parents.

Love is elusive, sought after, fought for. Some people spend all their lives seeking love, whereas others live almost completely deprived of it. Thousands of people work hard at maintaining a love relationship. Love can die a slow death never to be reborn again, but love can also grow and flourish with the passage of time. We write novels, songs, and plays about this powerful need. People fall in and out of love, but we have limited words to describe the actual concept of love. It is an abstract and relational concept characterized by feelings rather than words. How do you describe this magical feeling when the world seems brighter, life seems worthwhile, and happiness reigns supreme? When love flourishes, loneliness is not present as some silent company.

Love involves a relationship between two people, a relationship which is real as opposed to superficial, in which there is trust as opposed to suspicion and mistrust, and caring as opposed to selfishness. Individuals lower their defenses because there is less threat and one is not afraid to reveal strengths and weaknesses. Is this an adequate description? It is only a start; I am not so expert in love that I can provide a detailed description. I know how to feel the presence of love, and I must exert an effort to keep it from vanishing.

Love and belonging are found in genuine friendship. Where there is genuine caring, there is an intense relationship between two people. They complement each other's personalities and provide mutual emotional rewards that are quite different from the safe sentiments of group affection. People want to feel needed by someone, to fit as one whole piece in the puzzle of relationships. Very few individuals prefer to live in isolation without concern for belonging and affection. Most people strive to achieve some type of affectionate relationship within a family or a group. Some people will go to great lengths to achieve a true relationship. Some tolerate what they have, while others avoid reaching out and remain at the level of physical and security needs.

In our society there is a strong emphasis on all aspects of sexuality. Some people regard sexual and love relationships as synonymous. The values of many young people are confused as a result of a constant bombardment of movies, magazines, and ads that emphasize the importance of sexuality in everyday life. They have very little to model themselves after, since some parents preach one thing to their children and then practice the opposite. I think that the best relationship that two people can have is to be, first of all, the very best of friends. When there is sexual love in the relationship, then the ties can be even stronger; however, the needs are highly individualistic. Sexuality may not be an essential element in friendship or love, and it can even be seen as an obstacle in some situations. By itself it cannot prevent loneliness, as some people are led to believe. Sexuality alone cannot provide the kind of emotional tie that is so essential in true friendships. Some can only look upon sex as a temporary anesthetic against loneliness.

How do two people preserve the same feelings as years come and go? This is a difficult task. Life does not stand still. I often think that I knew all the answers when I was twenty. I now think how little I knew when I was thirty. I think of the changes in my life caused by values, experiences, and psychological growth. There were lonely times when I reached for a hand in the dark for some support. There were happy times when the world was incredibly beautiful, and life was miraculous.

Life does not stand still. It passes very quickly, from hour to day, from month to year. Two people must grow together, change their values, change their philosophies, and accept these changes. For love to flourish, open communication is needed between two people, as well as a total sharing of their feelings. This is probably much easier said than done. People often spend too much time talking and too little time listening. Such individuals are often stepping into a world of loneliness.

The transient nature of our population where people are new-comers rather than old-timers, where people lose their roots in family and neighborhoods has a negative effect on both children and adults. The need to belong is severed on several occasions. Unless they greatly disliked their environment, many children and adults feel a sense of loss when they move from old neighborhoods. There is a strong feeling that ties people to an area. They almost feel like animals with territorial rights in their homes and surrounding area. No matter how individual they may want to be or how alone they may want to remain, people are still social animals, since they depend on each other for existence. Remove that cord, the sense of belonging disappears. This feeling is not pleasant.

Our society is trapped on the level of wanting to belong and craving affection. We are not a warm, open society in which people are free to show their emotions with little inhibition. I think that the majority of people cling to this level, desperately searching for affection or feeling unsatisfied with the affection they are receiving. Again, I speak of giving and receiving as a two-way street. If you do not receive or give, you retreat into yourself. Not only do you feel alone and lonely, but you also feel frustrated. You do not react with anger as you would if you were denied physiological needs. I have seen societies in which there is a great deal of affection among families and friends. I have not seen too much evidence of this around me. I hope I am wrong.

As a reaction to the loss of affection and belonging, to the loneliness and aloneness, many young people form communes or join religious cults. This partially fulfills a need gratification that was not present in the family environment. The loneliness and alienation which results from superficial friendships, urbanization, and mobility are partly lessened by communal living. I think the same holds true for the rapid growth of encounter groups which many adults join. There is a sharing of feelings, a growth of closeness and intimacy that is not present in the world. At times, some of these people suffer intense loneliness when they return to the real world. They very quickly have to resort to their psychological cover-ups in order to survive in their environment.

There aren't many substitutes for a strong family. Remove the family and a part of the human foundation is lost. Where can you give and receive more affection and sense of belonging than in a closely knit family? It provides some of the strength that enables you to grow. There are no words that can describe a loving mother and father; you lose them and you lose part of your life. Human beings who have not experienced parental warmth have not experienced life.

THE NEED FOR APPROVAL

If the need for belonging and affection is satisfied, the individual moves to still higher needs in the hierarchy. These involve esteem and fall into two categories. One category is an individual's self-esteem. This includes the desire for competency, achievement, mastery, confidence, independence, and freedom. The second category concerns respect from other people. This includes concepts such as prestige, attention, status, reputation, acceptance, and appreciation. To simplify esteem involves the following questions: Do you feel good about yourself? Do others feel good about you?

As we move beyond needs for affection, we are developing

into individuals who can cope with many of life's problems. We suffer less and less from prolonged loneliness. We do not suffer if we are alone. Regardless of our wealth, our beauty, or our intelligence, when we reach this level of psychological growth, we are turning into a rare breed of person. We can still experience some loneliness, but we are more content with our lives and relationships. We are becoming individuals who are "doing our own thing" and becoming less concerned with all the variables affecting everyday life.

There is one rather interesting aspect of esteem needs which is absent to a large extent in our society. People are generally somewhat insecure, regardless of the type of work they do. They seem to hide in their own little shells and come up for fresh air once in a while. People who should feel secure and good about themselves often think the worst and dwell on their negative thoughts. Have you ever noticed that very few people can honestly compliment you on your appearance, your work, your achievements, or even the slightest positive thing that may fall your way? Or, if they do give compliments, their comments are positive on the surface but devoid of true sincerity. They cannot shake your hand because they are not genuinely happy for you. I hate feeble handshakes; they remind me of limp celery.

We love approval and attention, the two factors that greatly influence our behavior. We enjoy people noticing our presence. We feel warm inside when a person can honestly congratulate us for our good work or for some achievement. But how seldom this happens! During the past few years, I have received several grants for travel to conferences in countries outside Canada. I cannot recall one person in my area being really pleased with my achievements. In fact, the opposite is often true. I hear remarks such as "How did you manage that?" or "Do you know what I just finished doing?" In order to give approval and attention to others, you must feel secure as a person. You must have your feet planted firmly on the ground. You cannot be a lonely person searching for your soul. You must be able to walk with your head held high and be glad that you are you.

In his book *Working*, Studs Terkel describes numerous jobs and professions that take up at least eight hours a day for most people. I learned that a large percentage of the people hated what they were doing. They spent the time working only for money. How can this make people happy? How can they feel good about themselves when every hour seems an eternity and the world leans heavily on their shoulders? It takes courage to move out of a rut. One former neighbor was an engineer who totally disliked his work. He hated every minute of it; it affected his health and his relationships. He was a lonely person, grasping for some meaning in life. One day he quit his work and moved to a small town. Today he is making candles. He is doing something that he enjoys, regardless of the prestige or the amount of money he can keep in the bank. I would rather make enough money for essentials than reap large amounts of wealth and be miserable every hour of every day in the process. There must be more to life than money, heart attacks, and ulcers.

If self-esteem needs are not met, we have feelings of adequacy, strength, and self-confidence. If the needs are not met, we feel inferior, helpless, and weak. We can be discouraged, lonely individuals who feel life is really not what it is meant to be. We can compensate with neurotic behavior and eventually exhibit severe traumatic neuroses. This state does not lead to individual happiness but cripples our existence.

We must be realistic and in touch with our true experience. We cannot feel we are the greatest if in fact we are not. I have met men who think they are God's gift to humanity. I feel that they have overinflated egos that can burst at any time. There is also the danger of totally basing our self-esteem on the opinions of others. I think you can run out of steam if you wait for people to praise and reinforce you. Success should be based on competence and adequacy. Maslow feels that the most healthy self-esteem is based on deserved respect from others. We must applaud the scientist who discovers a cure for some disease as well as the rock star who provides joy to millions. Maybe we sometimes scream for the wrong person. Our silent cheers do not add to the needs of people who deserve the respect. But we are human, are we not?

In general, we human beings are thrown into a strange predicament. We want to feel good about ourselves, but we are often afraid to think along these lines. We usually spend more time dwelling on the negative rather than the positive aspects of our lives. The thoughts we have about ourselves strongly influence our train of thought and our behavior. If we feel good about ourselves, people often label us egotists or conceited. If we accept emotions, but behave in a manner that is contrary to our feelings, then we are not being honest with ourselves. Many of us are caught in the age-old dilemma of who we are and who we think we are.

We rely on people to give us some positive feedback and some encouragement as to our worth. One of the disappointing aspects of our society is the fact that people have great difficulty giving honest praise or honest evaluation. Many people can hand out the negative feedback with a fair degree of ease, but when it comes to something positive, it is quite a different story. I know numerous people who are successful in their line of work. They are almost hermits because others are not only unwilling to give due praise, but make numerous subtle jokes about their successes.

Why are people so unable to give? If a person is stuck on the level of needing affection, he is still trying to satisfy his want. He is unable to move up to the level of esteem needs. Unless he is honest with himself, he remains a person who does not have a good self-image. When he does not think the best of himself, his behavior will not reflect his thoughts. Sometimes he will put on a front that will attempt to hide most of his feelings. A person who is reserved is often unable to give or receive approval.

I never cease to be amazed by the aloofness of man. Often nonverbal clues show how one feels, even when lips remain tightly closed. I have known people who were talented, attractive, highly intelligent, and very successful in their work. Regardless of how great they were, they still needed the attention and the feedback that builds a sense of positive self-worth. Some of these people did not survive their late teens. I wonder what happened to their parents and teachers. Did they not notice the psychological disintegration of the individual? However, like others, they were probably dwelling on their own needs, quite oblivious to the needs of others around them. Deep down inside they were lonely people preoccupied mainly by their own dark world.

THE NEED
FOR SELF-ACTUALIZATION

If needs for love and esteem are met, man can move to the apex of the hierarchy of needs, namely self-actualization. What is meant by this need? Man becomes more and more what he is and is capable of being. To reach this state, man must grow and utilize his potential. Very few people are capable of achieving this level. I am often surprised that many of my students feel they are self-actualized at the age of twenty! Some people say this is "doing your own thing," but the idea is somewhat more complicated. If a person is self-actualized, he usually exhibits certain characteristics which distinguish him from others.

Self-actualized people tend to see life clearly, as it is and not how it should be. They tend to more objective and less emotional about their observations by not allowing their values, wishes, and hopes to cloud thier observations. They are often able to judge people correctly and see through the phoniness of individuals. When it comes to choosing a marriage partner, their selection is by no means perfect but above average.

These individuals have a clear perception of right and wrong. Confused and concealed realities of life are usually seen with greater speed and accuracy. Because of their position in the hierarchy, they can really listen and exhibit humility. They are aware that people can teach them something and that they are not huge storehouses of knowledge and experience. They possess some basic human quality of being themselves. Because of this child-like quality, there is no fear of ridicule from others. Many children can sing, paint, or dance without a great deal of instruction or planning. Self-actualized people are like these children.

Work is exciting and pleasurable, and the commitment to their work is essential for happiness and growth. Their work is done very well, but they also find time to be creative. Creativity is almost equal in meaning to self-actualization or full humanness. People who are creative exhibit characteristics such as flexibility, openness, courage, spontaneity, and humility.

Self-actualized people feel competent and adequate with a healthy self-respect. They have more self-knowledge than other people. They are highly independent, but still enjoy the company of others. They are very individualistic people, but also very loving and friendly. Life is controlled more by inner drives and natural needs than by the demands of society.

Finally, they form deep, close friendships with only a few

individuals. Such people can be tolerant of each other's shortcomings, but they dislike lying, dishonesty, or cheating in others. They have relationships that are not exploitive. Few people resemble them because they accept others regardless of their wealth, color, or creed. Self-actualized people are true human beings.

Are you such a person? Are you able to enjoy life with all of its aspects? Do you never tire of life? Do you have the time to enjoy a sunset or the color of an autumn leaf? Who are the self-actualized few? They are not only those at the apex of the needs hierarchy but also those few who are not lonely in the true sense of the word. Although they may have experienced loneliness in the past and are very much aware of the feeling in others, they are truly not lonely people in their present state.

How can we arrive at the level of self-actualization? No one can do the work for us. We in part have a fair amount of control over our lives. We have many options open to us. We can act or we can remain static. Many individuals are happy to be where they are and have no desire to grow and change. Thus we create the best possible self we can by being honest with our feelings and accepting the opinions of others we admire. When we feel good about ourselves, we can feel positively toward others. Following the proper sequence we continue to grow and grow. We never look back nor do we sigh with relief when we finally arrive. We continue to give to others as well as receive warmth and status. We move to the category of beautiful, happy people.

Finally, one cannot view the entire hierarchy of needs too precisely. Life does not follow a straight line. Most people in our society have partially satisfied most of their basic needs but still have some unsatisfied wants which, moreover, most influence their behavior. Once a need has been satisfied, it has little effect on human motivation. Basically, once a want is satisfied it is no longer a want.

The idea behind discussing needs is to make an individual aware of his basic motivation. It is important to realize where one stands in the hierarchy and to make an honest examination of the entire structure in terms of self. Unlike pure medicine, psychology offers few cures. However, needs must be examined in an attempt to explain an individual's behavior. It is a first step toward clarifying why we feel the way we do. We are left with questions such as, "What can we do about the situation?" and "Do we really have control over our existence?" I think we do.

We should not sit around and wait for something to happen by chance. Life is too short and too exciting. Why should we be hosts to the silent company?

four
Loneliness
from Childhood
to Midlife

Loneliness may keep company with anyone at any time or place. The possibility of its occurrence does not necessarily increase or decrease with age. Very young children as well as wealthy old people can lead very lonely lives. During all periods of life, loneliness can haunt us like some brooding ghost.

Certain stages during a lifetime may be more susceptible to loneliness, and we must be aware of the possibility of darker days when the silver lining appears to fade and vanish. Adolescence, the period of transition from childhood to adulthood with its traumas during courtship and the struggle for individuality, can be the first intensely lonely period. Because of the unbelievable rate of divorce in our society, a second experience with loneliness may occur when marriages begin to crumble and life takes a new, but not always exciting, adventurous twist. Finally, old age with its arthritis, nursing homes and pension checks, can lead to devastatingly lonely days, months, and years.

Life does not proceed along a beautiful tree-lined road with balanced sunshine and shade. The road of life is filled with turns, hills, and valleys. Moreover, our driving ability along this road is never very stable. At times we are able to maneuver the turns and bumps with a fair degree of skill; we emerge with only a few psychological scratches. Sometimes we miss a turn and in the process experience hurt and intense pain. Why didn't we know better? We often load ourselves with guilt and rationalizations to lessen our burden. We always ask, "Why me?"

I think we should listen to older people. As a young adult, I thought I knew everything, absolutely everything, and nobody could tell me what to do with my life. I thought I was too clever to be lectured to by my parents and grandparents. After all, they were old-fashioned and I was of another generation, and how could they understand, let alone help me?

Now that I am a bit older, and I hope wiser, I realize that reading, traveling and education help, but there is something to be said for experience. I can read about the depression years and imagine the hardships, but this is far removed from the person who actually experienced cold and hunger while riding on box cars in a world devoid of any warmth and hope. I can learn so much by carefully listening; wise words of advice become etched in my memory like annual rings on a stately tree.

As we grow from childhood to old age, we gain experience by learning to cope with our mistakes and to thrive on satisfactory decisions. Each stage of development adds to our total growth, but since we cannot turn back time, we cannot relive our mistakes or regain some growth that was missed. True, medical and psychological attempts to patch up human beings often help, but the net result is not a totally new person. The child who at six is a complete psychological mess has little chance of becoming a terrific self-actualized person. With the help of experts, he simply learns to cope.

CHILDHOOD

I would like to begin by sharing some ideas concerning childhood. Recently I read that in one year over two thousand children run away from home in our local city. This depresses me because we are looking at a number of very lonely human beings who left home for reasons other than a need for adventure. I have been amazed to learn how well children are able to cope with adults. They give grownups all the possible chances. When a situation becomes unbearable, some flee like frightened animals; others suffer in silence.

Childhood should not be a time for experiencing loneliness. It should be a time when life is ruled by make-believe, fairy tales, birthday parties, and sheer, unspoiled fun. In fact, childhood should be one of the best periods in one's life. These are the few years when there is no worry about taxes, food bills, creating impressions, and other related adult problems.

Unfortunately, situations do vary and many children are caught between loneliness and depression, between loneliness and tragedy. With mobility, family breakup, and parental struggle for a better standard of living, many children are simply existing rather than living. Like soldiers caught between two war fronts, they surrender or fight. One could write a volume about these tragedies, but what can we as adults do to help children cope with the winds of change?

ADULTS AND CHILDREN

An adult must genuinely love his child, not with words or gifts but with physical contact. A child must feel wanted by somebody who cares and treats him as a worthwhile human being. A child does not want to be physically or verbally abused. A parent or teacher can emotionally devastate a child with ridicule. What takes minutes to inflict can take years to mend.

You must take a child's feelings seriously. You must listen with all your strength. Show empathy. It is easy to ignore what a child is really trying to say by giving quick solutions to his problems. For example, Mary is very upset because her friend is moving to Toronto; they have been very close friends for several years. She is in tears as she relates her feelings to her mother. Mother can react by saying, "Oh Mary, you will find other friends. Jane isn't the only nice kid around," or she may respond by saying, "Mary, you're not a baby. Only babies cry. You aren't even hurt and there's no reason to cry just because Jane is moving to Toronto. Now just stop it!" Another way of responding could be, "Mary, you seem very upset about losing your friend. It is sad to have a close friend move away. I know you will miss her very much." With this remark, the mother is able to respond to Mary's problem. The child simply wants someone to understand how she feels.

We provide for a child's physical needs, but what about affection and status needs? We often grumble about the money we spend on food, clothes, and toys. However, the difficulty arises when we must give of ourselves. This is something that money cannot buy, but so necessary for a child who is to flourish in a demanding world.

We deal with adults when they commit various crimes, yet we do very little with adults who commit one of the more serious crimes, inflicting psychological injuries upon countless young people, injuries that wound and devastate the lives of so many children. There are thousands of children who are subjected to cruelty. Children should not be confined to mere survival. All of us should give this matter serious thought and take action to avoid pain and tears.

One of the striking features of modern society is that people can choose whether or not to have a child. Many couples are realizing that children may not fit into their life styles; this is not a selfish matter, but a realistic one. I think that we have progressed in our society when a couple can decide whether or not they want a child. Why produce another unwanted child into this world? Why should an innocent life experience the sheer hell of daily existence?

I hope that all parents are concerned about their child. Somehow it all works out if the parents have some warmth and some positive attitudes. However, knowing what to do with a child does not provide all the answers. A child psychiatrist could have children that are ready for the zoo. Simply because an individual knows what is in a textbook does not mean that he can apply this knowledge in everyday life. The problem is putting theory into practice. What one reads, and what one knows, and what one does do not always complement each other. It is amazing that children survive as well as they do.

Children today appear to know so much more than I did when I was their age. It seems that children have a sixth sense, so that they can perceive what I feel and know what I think. They are very good at nonverbal cues, since they do not clutter their feelings and their perceptions with irrelevant thoughts. Children are very realistic and can take a lot of problems in their stride; however, they are only human and can be pushed against a wall for a limited time.

Teachers and Students

As a former high school teacher, I have strong feelings about student-teacher relationships. I hope I am wrong, but many teachers view their work as a job, and the school as a place to teach academic subjects. Not all teachers are concerned with the learner, how he feels, what he thinks of himself, and how he sees the world. A teacher does not teach a subject; he teaches a child who is a worthy human being with all his strengths and weaknesses. A teacher can be an important person in a child's life, but it takes someone who is sensitive, not just academic. A smile goes further than a frown, a "Hi" goes further than silence. "Good try" leads to better results than "forget it." In school a student often gets very little attention and approval, so necessary for learning and growth.

On the other hand, I realize that teachers are not superhuman, but I feel they should try to reach as many young people as they possibly can. You can sometimes make some lonely child's life just a little brighter. You can have so much influence. It is worth a try.

I recall a group of high school students sharing some of their feelings with a psychologist. Many of the questions asked were related to their values and feelings. One question asked was, "Who would really miss you tomorrow if you died today?" Not one student mentioned that their teacher would miss them. I was terribly disappointed. One boy said the only one who would miss him would be his dog. Funny? Maybe, but also very sad.

What do we need in addition to love and empathy? We need communication. In fact, it might be the answer to the survival of human relationships. With a child, we must communicate with understanding; to learn this we must learn to listen carefully. Do not spend time giving a child big answers to small questions. Do not spend hours telling the child what not to do. Give advice when it is asked for. The child should know what he feels and not really why he feels this way. He is not a psychologist, and neither are we. The *why* may come later. What he feels can also be conveyed by nonverbal communication such as facial expressions. Place your emphasis, in terms of praise or disappointment, on the child's actions and not on him as a person. If Bill carries out the garbage, don't talk about his strength and power. Show your pleasure for Bill's work. If Susie spills her milk or breaks a cup, don't call her a clumsy ox. Direct your disappointment to the action, not to Susie as a person.

What Children Need

We should not force adulthood upon our children. We should not expect an eight-year-old to act like a twelve-year-old. We should allow children to be themselves and forget about growing up. Years pass very quickly, children pass from diapers to hopscotch, from kindergarten to junior high school. Why can't people enjoy their child regardless of their stage of development? We can hardly wait for the day when they are able to feed themselves, clothe themselves, make their own lunch, and sit without babysitters. Why can't we let children be children?

Next to affection, children need time to play. Play is a serious matter for all children, as important as good food and fresh air. We do not always allow time for play because there are chores to be done, as well as music lessons, swimming, ballet, hockey, gymnastics, and multiplication tables. I wonder how I survived childhood without any lessons outside of school! However, I remember the fantastic fun I had with my friends, rafting, making snow houses, and looking for crows' eggs.

Sometimes we expect our children to be good in everything. Others do not care if their children are even alive. In either case, children quickly intuit an adult's feelings. The pressure builds up, and they either revert to the world of loneliness and depression, or lash out against the world. In either case, the situation is a tragedy.

I wish that children could forget about being tough, or having fluffy hair and cute clothes. I wish that children could play with their dolls or their trains for years, instead of worrying about being too old or too mature for such activities. I wish that we could stop comparing children, by setting up models for others to follow. Why can't we let a child be an individual, someone unique? I wish that we could find time to spend with a child, to show him the beauty in a rainbow, to listen to the crunch of dry autumn leaves and to hear the wind whispering in the summer shade. I wish that adults could also be children at heart, instead of playing some role that is lost in the uncertainty of parenthood. I wish that children could enjoy every day of their lives as they grow through a very beautiful period in the human journey. The honesty, the innocence, and the sheer joy of being a child should be cherished every hour of the day.

Children and Their Peers

Peers are very important to a child. They provide the child some of the information that is necessary to build a picture of himself. If the feedback is positive, then the child feels good about himself; if it is negative, he usually fights back. Children are very cruel toward one another. Teasing, name-calling, and threats such as, "I will never play with you as long as I live!" are almost everyday experiences. I remember standing in the hallway in one of the schools where I taught. There was a new girl in the school and she very much wanted to join a group. As she approached a chattering foursome, one girl looked at her and said, "Just because you look like a banana, that doesn't mean you are one of the bunch!" I felt so sorry for the poor girl! What could she do? The feelings of rejection experienced by children can be devastating. Some children cannot verbalize or show their feelings; they keep them inside and suffer in silence.

The rejection one experiences because he is not included on a team, in a game, or at a party can lead to loneliness and sadness. These are the occasions when an adult must provide some of the reassurance that the child so desperately needs. A hug or a kind remark will usually see the child through the crisis. The unpleasant experience is soon forgotten and the person moves to the next crisis. The foundation for trust, affection, and total communication is developed at these times. If these feelings and trust continue, there is less chance that the child will turn to his peers, drugs, or alcohol for affection and recognition. If children feel good about themselves, they have the courage to say "no" without feeling rejected. This security can last a lifetime. Self-confidence leads to fantastic feelings.

When working with children, our eyes should be open, our ears attentive and our hearts receptive. Let us at least try to give our children a decent start. Let us avoid with all our strength creating the lonely feelings that will probably haunt them in later years. Let us satisfy the needs for belonging and affection our children require. This could be the best gift we can give them. Large sums of money cannot purchase this precious gift; only humans can provide it with their hearts.

Beyond Childhood

But children grow into young adults very quickly. They always want to appear grown-up, and before your very eyes, you see your child finishing school and wondering what to do with his life. What is in store for these young people? What can they expect to see in their twenties or thirties? Many hope they will be happily married, with beautiful children and a high paying job. This is not always the case.

C. Bryant in *Time Magazine* (April 28, 1975) describes the contributions of life-cycle scholars Roger Gould, psychiatrist at UCLA, Daniel Levinson, psychologist at Yale, and George Vaillant, psychiatrist at Harvard. Their work interests me a great deal. The reason may be that the application of their cycles to my own life seems to fit rather neatly. I can see the cycles applying to others as well. Furthermore, I think that life cycles relate to loneliness. Even though anyone at any age can be a prime candidate for loneliness, I feel that the adolescents, the middle-aged and the aged are three groups that can expect to encounter various degrees of loneliness in their lives.

Like some giant shadow, loneliness is always lurking near us and attempting to penetrate our life space. We run and it runs after us; it finds us when we are hiding. If we accept the idea that life consists of certain stages of development, growth, or just incidents, then we can be more prepared to meet our silent company, understand its presence, and find the means to cope with all the associated feelings.

CYCLE I:
ADOLESCENCE,
LEAVING THE FAMILY

The following poem was written by a high school senior who apparently committed suicide. It was given to me by a teacher in one of my college classes.

He always wanted to explain things, but no one cared.
Sometimes he would draw and it wasn't anything.
He wanted to carve it in stone or write it in the sky.
He would lie out in the grass and look up in the sky
And it would only be him and the sky and the things inside him that needed
*   saying.*
And it was after that that he drew the picture.
He kept it under his pillow and would let no one see it.
And when it was dark, and his eyes were closed, he could still see it
And it was all of him. And he loved it.
When he started school he brought it with him
Not to show to anyone, but just to have it with him like a friend
It was funny about school.
He sat at a square, brown desk.
Like all other square, brown desks.
And he thought it should be red.
And his room was a square, brown room
Like all the other rooms.
And it was tight and close. And stiff.
He hated to hold the pencil and chalk.
With his arm stiff and his feet flat on the floor, stiff.
With the teacher watching and watching.
The teacher came and spoke to him.
She told him to wear a tie like all the other boys.
He said he didn't like them.
And she said it didn't matter.
After that they drew.
And he drew all yellow and it was the way he felt about morning.
And it was beautiful.
The teacher came and smiled at him.
"What's this?" she said. "Why don't you draw like Ken's drawing?"
"Isn't that beautiful?"
After that his mother bought him a tie.
And he always drew airplanes and rocketships like everyone else.
And he threw the old picture away.

And when he lay alone looking at the sky,
It was big and blue and all of everything.
But he wasn't anymore.
He was square inside, and brown,
And his hands were stiff.
And he was like everyone else.
And the thing inside him that needed saying didn't need it anymore.
It had stopped pushing.
It was crushed. Stiff.
Like everything else.

A High School Senior

Somewhere between childhood and adulthood we find the surprise of adolescence. We see the personality of a child that is in the body of an adult. The adolescent needs to be loved and wants to be independent, but when he is allowed self-direction, he has very little idea of what direction to take. Give adolescents love but there is little certainty that it will be accepted or returned. They possess physical and sexual powers without the experience or knowledge to use them. Adolescents live in our complex, structured society whose goals, values, and answers are understood with great difficulty. The transition to adulthood is not an easy task; it is a trying period where individuals try to understand and be understood.

Developing Sexuality

Adolescence begins as a biological phenomenon with sexual maturation as its main theme. The appearance of pubic hair and the enlarging sex organs in boys are often the signs that mark the attainment of physical sexual maturity. At this stage adolescents are capable of biological reproduction. The physical and maturational changes also reflect the increase in hormone production, which in turn affects the growth spurt. However to the alarm of many individuals, different parts of the body mature at different times and rates. Young adults quickly learn what the ideal body types are. Any deviation from the ideal body profoundly influences their self-image and peer approval.

In their sexuality and intimacy, adolescents reflect society's new openness with regard to sexual behavior. The media helps to imply that sexual behavior is personal rather than moral. For the majority, experimentation in sex roles does not reflect emotional maturity. They have all the essential parts but many don't seem to understand how the parts work, or what goes with what. Pressures do exist. The boy who has never kissed a girl feels somewhat deflated when he hears some of the macho types talk about their sexual conquests. Are today's youth any more promiscuous than the youth of former times? I think not.

The Search for Identity

Adolescence is a search for identity. It is a time when a person begins to think about himself in terms of who, what, and why. The examination and reexamination of one's identity is a major developmental task. Ideally, with success and the help of adults around him, each begins to feel more and more worthy as an individual. He experiences a sense of well-being and of self–worth. With the growth of self, gender role, and maturity, one begins to narrow his vocational choices. For many males, sex roles and vocational roles tend to interact. For the adolescent male, his competence in a vocational role is certain to be a dimension of his identity as is his masculinity in the sex role.

From the standpoint of social relations, parents and the home environment have lasting influences on youth. Parents affect basic decisions with regards to occupation, independence, and the self-control that one is likely to exhibit. How often I have seen parents blunder in this area! Some hold on to their adolescent's shoe strings well beyond the twenties. Some want to know their son's or daughter's whereabouts almost every hour. Some subject their offspring to incredible pressures to achieve in music, academics, or sports. In other social classes, adolescents are told to get out and get a job. Money and cars tend to be high priorities. I know cases where young men were devastated by parental insistence to study engineering or medicine instead of ballet or art. The inability to please and associated depression sometimes leads to suicide.

Peer Pressure

Peer influence on the formation of an adolescent's identity is crucial. Often friendship moves from sharing activities to psychological sharing. For many this is the start of heterosexual companionship. Many individuals derive their self-worth, values, and goals from other peers. Groups and cliques usually form. The adolescent learns what his status is within the group. Cliques resemble society; both have their pecking order. Similar characteristics bind individuals to a group. For some, there is no binder.

Youth gives way to the fantasy of adulthood. Young people are breaking away from the family and beginning to find their peers useful allies. However, peer groups tend to impose group beliefs upon the person. Many friendships are brittle, and disagreement by a friend tends to be viewed as a betrayal. Some of our first serious romances occur in this stage, with the frequent beginning and ending of love affairs. Many are floating in a sea of humanity without an anchor or a helping hand. When friendships are in transition, and a love affair comes to a sad end, what does the person feel? Loneliness, intense loneliness, with despair and sadness. Do you remember when you were unable to sleep because you experienced this intense feeling? The hours crawl by. You close your eyes but your mind remains active. Life looms ahead of you like some high, formidable mountain. Pain surrounds you. You silently cry for help.

Adolescent Alienation

Young people feel a certain amount of alienation from themselves. This means that they keep their thoughts and feelings apart. Furthermore, it is not cool to show feelings. The image they try to portray is one of no emotion, dependency, or enthusiasm. Boredom seems to be one word that describes so many of our young people. Motivation is missing in both the homes and schools.

In order to release their feeling, many seek a "turn on." A good example of this behavior is found at rock concerts. The loud music and mass socialization combine to permit them to behave in a manner that would not be highly acceptable on a one-to-one basis. Some turn to drugs and alcohol as a temporary or permanent escape.

Youth also experiences alienation from others. Young people not only move away from their own feelings, but from others as well. Many are afraid to risk social involvement, and because they are not sure of themselves, their social skills are unsophisticated. However, many individuals feel they are in a bind. They can be uninvolved, feel no pain, and never cry. But on the other hand, they cannot remain isolates either; they risk experiencing disappointment and hurt.

Finally, youth experiences alienation from culture, values and tradition. Many look upon religion and politics with apprehension. They do not feel institutions provide too many answers. In addition, adults do not always set the best example for their children. How can you warn a son about cheating when you pat yourself on the back every time you cheat someone out of a dollar? The entire uncertainty of the future poses incredible pressures on the young adult. What can they plan or believe in when they listen to the news and there is very little joy in the message?

Unfortunately, youth turns to mass media as a source of information. It follows heroes like Bob Dylan or the Bionic Man. Television tells them what to do, when to do it, and why it should be done. Peers are also an excellent source of information. They feel safe to ask each other for advice. Schools are third on the list as sources of information. A good staff can contribute to the welfare of many students. If the school is a huge jungle where every student is known by number only, then the pupils feel that no one cares about their welfare.

In general, alienation is related to emptiness and feelings of worthlessness. Whether it involves the self and self-concept, or relationships with others, the usual result is a feeling of loneliness. If any words describe the youth of today, "the lonely generation" would probably be most appropriate.

Other Aspects of Adolescence

Benjamin Disraeli said that youth is a blunder, manhood a struggle, and old age a regret. There is much truth in this statement. Even though many seeds of behavior are sown in infancy and childhood, it is never too late to understand or at least to attempt to appreciate the problems faced by man. Again, I particularly think it is essential for parents and teachers to try to understand how youth thinks and feels.

Adolescents today are probably no different from adolescents in the past. The world, however, has changed and poses many problems for today's youth. This is not to say that youth in the past did not have any problems. When I think of the trauma of war, and the total uncertainty of what the result would be, today's young people have problems that are minor in comparison to what faced youth in 1940.

What are some other characteristics of youth that may help us to understand them? Moving from a child's reasoning, the adolescent enters a stage of logical thinking. Probably only half today's youth is able to operate at a level of abstract thought. Whereas many children must learn to think in concrete terms, this is not the case for sixteen-year-olds. Basically, they do acquire good intellectual skills enabling them to see discrepancies. Faith in all authority is questioned. Emotional reliance upon religion, ethics, and morality is challenged. At the same time, youth tends to be idealistic; they think in ideal rather than in practical terms. When the ideal and the real world are in conflict, they experience anxiety and frustration.

I think that if people were asked whether they would like to relive their adolescence, most would give an emphatic "No." The acne, the change in voice, the cute girl refusing a dance in the high school gymnasium, and the traumatic body changes are features that add to feelings of inadequacy and to a lowering of self-confidence.

All child-parent relationships are in transition but the emotional dependence upon parents remains for a long time. In fact, if the parent-child relationship is a good one, I believe there is some degree of emotional dependence upon the parents during an entire life span. It is during this life cycle that the promise of finding oneself and losing oneself are very closely related. For example, society can stamp a label on the individual, such as "lazy worker," "rotten person," or "failure," even though this behavior may be exhibited only temporarily and the individual feels otherwise.

As they constantly search for assurance, youth will sometimes seek out some significant adults who can be very special to them. These adults are selected for the meaning they convey as the adolescent experiences role development. In addition to parents, teachers, church leaders, or social workers play important roles. These relationships can alleviate some loneliness and enable adolescents to develop healthier psyches. All individuals must be accepted for their strengths. When their awareness of what they think they are coincides with the impression conveyed to others, they will gain a sense of identity; however they will often continue to act in a manner that reflects who they think they are rather than who they really are.

ADOLESCENTS AND ADULTS

Because of the transitory nature of this life cycle and because of the many tragic results found during this period of growing up, I once again beseech parents, teachers, and other adults who play important roles in the lives of youth, to try and understand them. What can we do? We must respond in much the same way as I described in reaching out to children. Respect the feeling of each individual; do not fight fire with fire. Be sympathetic and lend your shoulder when it is needed. Take time to listen. Communicate your concern. Don't let things get out of hand, because it is a long journey back. At times we do not reap the benefits of our trials and tribulations. Why give your sixteen-year-old a car when he does not have the experience to handle it? How many news bulletins have we heard where cars were sliced in half when they hit light poles? Do you want to carry guilt and grief all your life?

The path to human growth is often a rough one. If only youth had someone to talk to, much of their behavior, which we might consider strange or weird, would disappear or at least diminish. They do not want you to solve their problems; they want you to care with all your heart. They want to use you as a model. Try and live up to that expectation. Youth wants you to set limits, even though they may resist your authority. Do not give in. Be consistent. Praise and reinforce whenever the situation demands this. Give a big hug; it goes a long way. Slow down a bit, and don't always be in a rush. Notice that your boy has changed during the past few months; he is starting to shave and grow fuzzy sideburns. You smile and you receive a smile in return. Must one say more?

To summarize, the life cycle of leaving home involves the transition from childhood to adulthood. The period is marked by numerous crises, including seeking self-identity, choosing a vocation, experiencing romance. For the first time the individual will have a pretty fair idea of his intellectual and physical abilities. The majority will return to their peers for some guidance, support, and approval. Home influences never die if there have been good relationships between family members to begin with. Some parents fear that they are losing some of their grip on the child, and this is probably realistic.

Young people in this stage of development need the attention of adults. When we consider the high suicide and accident rate among members of this age group, the seriousness of growing up hits us with full force. Tragedy knows no barriers. The rich and the beautiful, as well as the poor and the not-so-beautiful, have feelings. We adults must help adolescents develop confidence, so that a strong, positive self can emerge and flourish. Even though some of the foundations have been established for many individuals, they still require support from significant adults. The feedback we provide can avert much of the loneliness and sadness that many young people may experience. The support that we can give is not a remedy, but it can help overcome some of life's hurdles. In this world of money, fast living, and materialism, we often forget someone who should be close to us. We can avoid tragedy if we really care for our children.

We must always attempt to keep in touch with our young people, and treat them as unique individuals. Teachers must give of themselves to as many pupils as possible. We often look at the quiet boy in the back row as the model of what a student should be; however, he may be the loneliest person in the room. Even though it takes effort on our part, giving and reaching out is truly worthwhile. After all, what is our purpose in life? What sets us apart as human beings?

CYCLE II:
REACHING OUT
(AGES 23–28)

Touch but my lips with those fair lips of thine,
Though mine be not so fair, yet are they red,
The kiss shall be thine own as well as mine.

What seest thou in the ground? Hold up thy head:
   Look in mine eyes, there thy beauty lies;
   Then why not lips on lips, since eyes in eyes?

Art thou ashamed to kiss? then wink again;
And I will wink; so shall the day seem night;
Love keeps his revels when there are but twain;
Be bold to play, our sport is not in sight:
   These blue-vein'd violets whereon we lean
   Never can blab, nor know not what we mean.

W. Shakespeare, *Venus and Adonis*

Consider this period of growth one of the better cycles of life. Some of the growing pains found during adolescence have disappeared, some of the surprises in terms of physical development have been established, and the foundations have been laid during the past twenty years. Adulthood has been reached.

Experimentation in various roles has established some of your strengths and weaknesses. If you are honest with yourself, you can now accept yourself as a person with positive and negative qualities. You step up to the next level in life with some confidence. Probably in this cycle you will fall in love as you never fell before. Yes, you did have some intense emotional experiences during your adolescence, but they were mainly to discover who you really were. Were you truly as cute as your aunt said you were? Did your football player physique turn on every female in the country? As you gave your last performance in the school play, was there a chance you would soon star opposite Jane Fonda? Now, whether actor or aspiring medical student, you scan the horizon for the real slot in society where you are able to work and grow. After all, you are special and have much to contribute to all of us.

Every phase of life has its problems, for life cannot exist without painful decisions. What agony we experience when we have several roads we can follow, and must decide which one to choose. To make matters worse, in life there is very little turning back. Time is a one-way street. You make the wrong turn and you live with the consequences. However, I see this cycle as one where loneliness falls to a low level, after reaching a fairly high peak in the previous cycle. Of course, there could be very lonely times in store. Your six-year engagement comes to a sad end as your fiancée runs off with another. Anger can be followed by loneliness.

How well I remember my twenties! There seemed to be so much time and energy. I was teaching high school, and enjoyed the work a great deal. Every day I drove around in my new Ford convertible. I had no debts and earned almost four hundred dollars a month. During some of those years I was living on the West Coast. I remember the rain coming down in sheets during the winter months, after the beautiful fall days when the rays of the sun seemed to provide warmth so reminiscent of summer. I remember the years of skiing when I finally took the ski-lift up a high slope and froze at the top, barely able to see the bottom of the ski run. I remember spring nights with the whole world in bloom and the joy of smelling the fresh greenness of the new grass. The scent in the air was almost intoxicating. Is this what they call getting high? I remember my friend and I going for a car ride with our girlfriends. We drove into a beautiful wooded, quiet, country road. The music was fantastic; we got out of the car and danced on the road. The trees were freshly leaved, the air was balmy and, of course, the entire beauty was encased in love. The twenties were a great period in my life.

Gould, Levinson, and Vaillant found the dominant feature of the twenties to be the search for personal identity and the ability to develop intimacy. This is an age of reaching toward others. It is a time of togetherness and a time for marriage. This is the typical age group that you see in the "Diamonds are Forever" advertisement in the paper. We see pictures of a couple looking fondly into each other's eyes or some boy beaming as his girl gazes at her newly acquired gem.

Erik Erikson calls this phase of life the acquisition of a sense of intimacy and solidarity, and avoidance of a sense of isolation. With childhood ending, it is now time to settle to the task of full participation in the community, to enjoy life with adult liberty and responsibility. The twenties are a time for studying, working at a career, and establishing social relationships with the opposite sex. This involves a psychological readiness to share mutual trust and procreation.

Living Alone Versus Marriage

We look at this cycle of life as a period of love and work. Efforts are directed toward improving and interpreting patterns of cooperation with allowances for competition, and for patterns of friendships and love. If the efforts are not satisfied in marriage, then the individual must find solutions elsewhere, perhaps in disjointed love associations, or in a more total immersion in one's work.

A dilemma can arise in some individuals who are contemplating marriage. Years ago, if a person was single, people saw him as being somewhat strange. For many it was difficult to accept the fact that a person chose to live alone. In fact, there was, and probably still is, subtle pressure from parents, siblings, and friends to marry. After all, some still believe that being *alone* represents the total symbol of loneliness, true loneliness with no one to share an intimate relationship.

Today we tend to accept a person's decision to live alone, and to be happy in his aloneness. He is not using some form of defense mechanism by explaining that the right person did not come along. Many people realize that to be married just for the sake of being married is certainly not the answer. Many look at their friends who terminated their marriages and are burdened with financial as well as emotional problems; they decide that this is not the route to take. Many leave the option to marry open. After all, one never really knows when the chemistry may begin to work. However we tend to think that the marriageable people are spoken for when we reach our thirties, and there are only leftovers to choose from.

I do not feel very strongly about aloneness versus marriage. Like most experiences in life, both have good and bad qualities. However, I feel that if you are alone, you do not necessarily experience loneliness and you have freedom which is second only to money. You may be that "alone" person, or you may know some friends or acquaintances who are in this situation. They can be truly happy people.

Marriage is a fantastic institution if the marriage is good. You may disagree, but I feel that the number of truly good marriages are indeed very rare. When I stop to think of the dozens of married couples I know, the majority are simply financial and social conveniences. There is nothing really good and, on the other hand, nothing really bad about the relationships. For many, life stays on one plateau. Children come along, a house is acquired, and life goes on with its daily routine of working, eating, watching television, and sleeping. Acquaintances looking in from outside view the relationship as being terribly monotonous. Sometimes, one or both partners wake up and feel they want no part of it; others wake up but close their eyes to the situation. Some never really wake up.

Marriage is not a solution for loneliness. Marriage probably does enable one to alleviate some loneliness, but it is total fallacy to look upon a married person with envy; that individual can be the loneliest creature walking the earth.

There are so many variations of marriage that I would not even begin to describe them. In fact, no two people are alike and thus no two marriages are alike. Each marriage is a union between two people. If it works for them, then nothing else matters. Nothing is gained by calling it a "good" or "bad" relationship.

Love and Marriage

Since Cycle II is when love and intimacy occur, let us examine love and marriage in more detail. There are many definitions of love, from dictionary to Biblical descriptions. It is a term that is used by everyone day after day, but we tend to generalize and interpret the concept from our own frame of reference. Love can mean standing and waiting in the rain for one hour. It may mean loneliness and emptiness in the absence of one person, or it may also mean ecstatic joy and boundless energy. We think we know when it is found, when it blooms, and when it dies. Love is a passionate friendship.

In *Rilke on Love and Other Difficulties,* J.L. Mood discusses Rainer Maria Rilke's classic food for thought regarding love. I feel it is something that every young person in his twenties keeps high on his list of priorities. Many think that falling in love is a terrific emotional experience, which it is, but the ecstasy can quickly fade if there is nothing else. Making love is not the same as love, and neither is whispering sweet nothings in someone's ear.

No, this is not what love is. Rilke says that there is scarcely anything more difficult than to love one another. Love is something very difficult to achieve. Young people are often not prepared for such a difficult task. We, as a society, have tried to make this relationship into something easy and fun, and claim that everyone is able to love. This is not so. Many people fling themselves at each other impatiently and in haste. This is followed by dissension, disorder, disunity, and confusion. Two people begin to treat each other with intolerance. In this state of confusion, two people become impatient, then what is dead cannot be clung to.

But human relationships are not all dark, crumbling, and decaying. There exist relationships which are almost unbearably happy. These exist between two persons who are very complete, very balanced, very beautiful people in their own right. Many people cannot achieve this type of relationship, but if they know their own selves, they can prepare for love and slowly grow toward happiness. There is a time when they are only beginners in love, and are like apprentices who make mistakes. Thus one must learn to love, and like all learning there must be patience, mistakes, some aloneness, and some loneliness. The goal is not for two people to become one; it is becoming oneself in a partnership. It is an inducement to maturity and growth.

What about the institution of marriage? Rilke maintains that we do not expect a single person to be happy and are surprised if a married person is not happy. Along with happiness, one might add that marriage also lessens loneliness. But it is not marriage per se that fends off loneliness, buy rather the availability of some emotional attachment. Empty marriages without emotional involvement are not a good defense against loneliness. There are nonmarital relationships that provide secure attachment, thus it is the attachment rather than the marriage that is important.

A good marriage is not a quick union, a tearing down of boundaries, but a relationship in which each person is a guardian of his self. Basically, total togetherness between two people is almost impossible. The tighter the bind, the smaller the chance for individuality, until each person is deprived of his freedom and development. Thus, there is distance even between two people who are very close. It is next to impossible to share ourselves completely with others. In meaningful relationships, we must be able to experience closeness while retaining our individuality.

We must experience solitude and room to breathe in a good relationship. We must have this distance in order to see the other person as well as ourselves. We must help ourselves before we can help others; trying to change the other is wrong. Marriage or partnership is a means of strengthening ourselves, and if the other person grows with us, the union is good. Obviously such relationships are difficult to achieve, and for this reason I feel there are few marriages that are truly fantastic.

I have heard couples talk about "working at their marriage." They feel they must keep it in mind and work at the relationship in order for it to survive. I question whether this is necessary in a good marriage. Do we really work when we are lost in play? Do we call a pleasurable experience "having to work"? If constant effort is required to make a relationship last, I question the quality of the relationship. What is fun, mutual and enjoyable should not require constant work.

In summary, we should not consider loneliness from the point of view of being married or single. We should not assume that because we see a man with a wife and four children that he lives a happier life than the man who lives alone in a three-room apartment. Furthermore, no matter what decision we make in terms of being alone or married, each has its positive and negative characteristics. Certainly, we should not marry simply out of fear of living alone nor with the idea that the presence of another person will somehow lessen the presence of the silent company. Since love is somewhat difficult to achieve, and since a marriage takes only a few minutes, the two do not always operate on the same plane. Perhaps we should first look at ourselves, our growth, our positive and negative characteristics, and know them well before we jump into a marriage, and perhaps into a loneliness more intense than we have ever experienced. Finally, we must be sure of our ability to love, to love ourselves and others. This is a period in life when we must be honest with our feelings. We must listen to them very carefully and learn.

CYCLE III:
QUESTIONS, QUESTIONS
(AGES 29–34)

When we two parted
In silence and tears,
Half-broken hearted,
To sever for years,
Pale grew thy cheek and cold,

Colder thy kiss:
Truly that hour foretold
Sorrow to this!

The dew of the morning
Sunk chill on my brow;
It felt like the warning
Of what I feel now.
Thy vows are all broken,
And light is thy fame:
I hear thy name spoken
And share in its shame.

They name thee before me,
A knell to mine ear;
A shudder comes o'er me—
Why wert thy so dear?
They knew not I knew thee
Who knew thee too well:
Long, long shall I rue thee
Too deeply to tell.

In secret we met:
In silence I grieve
That thy heart could forget,
Thy spirit deceive.
If I should meet thee
After long years,
How should I greet thee?
With silence and tears.

   Byron, "When We Two Parted"

Researchers tend to agree that for many individuals a crisis generally develops around the age of thirty. Life begins to look more painful and difficult; there is more self-reflection. There are questions asked such as, "What is life all about?", or "Why can't I be accepted for what I am and not what others such as my boss, my spouse, or society expect?" An active social life tends to decline during this period. For those who married in their twenties, there is a decline in marital satisfaction and the spouse is often viewed as an obstacle rather than as an asset. Marriage becomes particularly vulnerable to infidelity and one can experience their marriage slowly weakening. Thus, not only does one see many friends going separate ways but one's own marriage slowly deteriorating as well.

After adolescence, many lonely people find themselves in Cycle II. The joy of finding a partner, shopping for furniture, celebrating the first anniversary, and the great joy of having the first child is now in the past. Life has had its high and low periods, but now it tends to be more on the decline. Every day tolerance seems to hit lower and lower depths until one day any love that remains dwindles away. One is left with empty walls. Not even the house, the car, or the children seem to give one a great deal of uplift. One slowly settles into a period of loneliness that gnaws at every thread that holds life together. It grips one's emotions, and mingles with anger, guilt, and fear.

The other day I heard a friend talking about her parents. She shuddered at the advice her mother gave her regarding men. Her mother believes that any man is better than no man at all. Some believe that any marriage is better than no marriage at all. Such individuals are extremely limited in viewpoint and personal depth. People do make mistakes, but no one can live his life over again. A few lucky people learn from their mistakes, whereas others operate on a trial-and-error basis and hope for the best.

Marriage in Crisis

I must emphasize that I am considering people in general. Obviously what I am discussing would not hold true for a person who is marrying at the age of thirty-one or fifty. Nor does it mean that he will experience much the same life pattern as does the thirty-year-old who married when he was twenty-one. I cannot say that the person who marries for the first time at forty is more mature and knows what life is all about. I do not believe that one who remarries for the second or third time necessarily knows all the answers either. It is to be hoped that you won't repeat mistakes that you made in the past, and yet life patterns often do not change. If you are marrying for the third or fourth time, I would advise that you take a very critical look at yourself and your motives. How much experience does one person really need to survive? Most people learn by others' mistakes. You are a loser if you do not learn from your own mistakes.

Because this stage of life is highlighted by marital turmoil, I might add that there is no easy or creative way to approach separation or divorce. Maybe Hollywood provides some of the answers in real life or in movies. But since most of us are not in Hollywood circles, we cannot treat the event as a carefree, happy occasion.

Regardless of what happened during the married years, separated life contributes to feelings of anger, guilt, and loneliness. When children are involved, the situation compounds itself. The marital situation will correlate with the effects of separation. If the marriage was very bad, then each person will probably experience more relief than hostility. If the relationship during marriage was not terrible, anger and frustration may be exhibited by one of the partners. Along with some sense of relief, one goes through several stages of emotions, everything from intense hate to intense self-pity. The complete reorganization of one's life along with the search for new friends can lead to some of the loneliest hours in a person's life. Some vow they will never attempt another marriage as long as they live. Others run into a new relationship as quickly as their heels can carry them. If one partner has someone he can turn to, the separation becomes easier. The other person is able to absorb and share some of the pain. If one had no close relationship outside of marriage, he feels the pain and the loneliness for many silent hours and days.

Careers in Crisis

Other than marital situations, people in this cycle can experience degrees of loneliness due to problems at work and all the pressures surrounding the grasp for dollars. It is said that if a man does not start to settle down by the age of thirty-four, his chances of forming a reasonably satisfying life are quite small. There is a fair degree of truth in this saying. I am not certain if thirty-four is the magic age but during the first half of the thirties an individual should have his career fairly well established. There is a strong feeling of upward mobility in this stage of life. Striving for some order and stability, the person faces fairly severe cognitive and emotional strains.

I know an individual who recently separated from his wife and who was never happy with his work. He moved from one institution to another searching for the right position. Somehow the search seemed to be in vain. I spent one evening with him discussing his situation. Since people tend to react to him in a somewhat negative fashion, I decided to be very honest and point out some of his basic flaws as I saw them. What is the point of smiling and saying one thing while thinking another? Needless to say, the air was heavy. He burst into tears when the going was tough. I felt great empathy toward him. Deprived of a relationship which had lasted for fifteen years and lacking any job security, a man becomes a mere skeleton. I thought he had to come to grips with his own self and his own behavior before he could adequately cope with his environment. The constant moving in search of the Holy Grail just does not aid human growth; in fact, it usually adds to a great deal of frustration. My acquaintance is the classic example of a person who is intensely lonely.

At any period in one's life, job security is very important. Even when marriage relationships are good, the constant frustration associated with work, the quest for promotions, or merely coping with the work one has, can severely erode human relationships. To add to the problem, I think the majority of people work because they need the money to survive. The number of people who truly enjoy their work and would place it ahead of the amount of money earned form a small minority. Even though one theoretically settles into some meaningful work in his early thirties, I have high respect for an individual who changes jobs or professions. A rolling stone gathers no moss, but it may prevent heart attacks. Many professional people feel they have invested too much time, money, and education to turn back. I cannot imagine that every doctor and lawyer is simply mad about his work. There could be a great needlepoint artist somewhere in that crowd!

The Crisis of Failure

The overall hurt that can result in this stage of life is usually the result of failure. I think that failure and loneliness are very close friends. The child who fails to make the team can experience intense loneliness; he needs the support of an adult at such a time. The adolescent who fails in the realm of friendships and academics can experience hours of loneliness. By the time an individual reaches his mid-thirties, there are several well-established patterns of life that account for many of his waking hours. For example, a typical male spends a good deal of his time at work, as a husband, a father, or a friend. On the other hand, the typical female spends a great deal of her time earning money besides being a homemaker, a wife, a mother, or a friend. Generally speaking, the waking hours are spent at work or in some relationship role.

If a person experiences failure in only one area, such as work, then the net result is frustration and loneliness, but when there is failure in both one's work and in one's relationships, then the insecurity, pain, and loneliness hit with full force. Failure is very unpleasant because of the feelings it creates. The loneliness and depression associated with life's problems can only be overcome by one's internal strength. As you hold on to life, you should experience some solitude so you can think and begin a slow psychological climb upward. When you are flat on your back, you have no other way to go but up. When you finally emerge from the experience, you can be a greater person than you were before. The slow climb upward will be associated with less pain and loneliness. Life is often accompanied by heartache, fear, and frustration. I wonder if it is possible to experience life without the hurt that we inflict upon each other. But, after all, we are human, are we not?

But wait! Your problems are only beginning. Many men reach a crisis during their late thirties or early forties which is often referred to as the "male menopause." Others see it as "midlife crisis." Call it what you will, it reminds me of a second adolescence with its problems of identity, sexuality, and accompanying degrees of fear, guilt, and loneliness.

five
Loneliness from Midlife to Old Age

It is very difficult to refer to ages when we talk about the first half, the second half, or even the middle part of the human journey. There are thirty-year-old individuals who are mentally, physically, and socially like men of sixty. There are people in their fifties and sixties who are in the prime of their lives; their work, intellect, and social relationships are at their peak. Whatever the age and the individual differences, the past has considerable influence on present behavior.

We may not be smarter, better looking, or more socially competent when we reach forty, but we are certain that we are chronologically older. Being older has both positive and negative characteristics. Life itself does provide us with experiences that usually make us somewhat wiser, but it is worthwhile to listen to older people. Having traveled part of the journey, they have experienced some of the rough parts of the road, and are able to give us some advice. Physically, many of us tend to lose our shapes. We have a few more creases on our faces and we begin to sport a weathered look. In itself simply growing older is not a frightening experience. What is frightening, however, is seeing one big vacuum around us.

I imagine that many people do not like the idea of having to grow old, because they fear old age. Many are thinking of retirement, but when the time comes, they are unable to handle the freedom. Some save money when they are young, but do not spend it when they are old. Young people want more time and money. As with most things in life, we win some and lose some. However, one thing is certain; as we get older, we do not seem to have the energy which most of us had when we were younger. I recall when I was in my twenties I could stay up all hours of the night, catch a couple of hours of sleep, and then teach all day. I cannot cope with an abundance of activity in my present stage of life. If I have a late night, my body tells me to forget the eleven o'clock news and get some rest. I simply get tired more easily.

I arbitrarily choose forty as some division in the life cycles. If our life span stretches into the seventies, then the rationale becomes more obvious. If the journey through the first part of life was a rather smooth one, then there is a better chance for smoothness in the second half of the journey. In general, the pattern of life which has been established does have a bearing on the second half. Turbulent, unsettling, and traumatic years in the twenties and thirties usually have a profound effect on how a person will behave in his forties, fifties, and even sixties.

If we look at the general variables that affect life, the second half is probably smoother for the majority of the people. Many of the decisions regarding life have been made and certain life styles have been established. However, there is still one major hurdle that faces all of us, namely, the problem of old age. Let us examine what the second part of life has in store for us.

CYCLE IV: MIDLIFE CRISIS (AGES 35–43)

To laugh often and love much;
to win the respect of intelligent persons and the affection of children;
to earn the approval of honest critics and endure the betrayal of false friends;

> *to appreciate beauty;*
> *to find the best in others;*
> *to give of yourself without the slightest thought of return;*
> *to have accomplished a task;*
> *to have played and laughed with enthusiasm and sung with exaltation;*
> *to know that even one life has breathed easier because you have lived.*
> *This is to have succeeded.*

Anonymous

The second major upheaval after the adolescent stage of development usually comes in the midlife male menopause period. Sometimes it is referred to as the "dirty thirties" or "midlife crisis." If you managed to survive the wounds left by loneliness in the earlier stages, your body begins to suffer a new surge of loneliness that not only reopens old wounds but makes your psyche resemble a battlefield. You reach new levels of emptiness that only inner strength and hopefully the warmth of a few others can help you to withstand the turbulence of existence. Like a mighty oak, you will survive. Visibly shaken by the storm, you will emerge a newer, stronger man. You will be ready for greater heights.

No two of us are alike. Some of us are able to bear the storms of life rather bravely. We endure the shaking for a period of time but are able to reorganize and start life anew. Other weaker souls can be totally uprooted. When the calm finally falls, they lie bleeding and silently crying for help. But nature is never fair; man is not created equally.

Having gone through the turbulent thirties personally, and having seen numerous males around me who either are or were in crisis, leaves little doubt in my mind that midlife crisis does occur for many men. It is as real as day and night. However, one is a fool to sit around, breathlessly waiting for the storm to hit. You do not go to bed and wake up the next day feeling strange. You become different after a series of events. It is to be hoped that you have the strength to become the person you would like to be.

I am not implying that our lives can be compared to that of a butterfly. It is true we both start from an egg, and the caterpillar might be compared to our childhood when we eat our parents' pocketbooks out of existence. The pupa stage can be compared to midlife when we have the possibility to emerge into butterflies or maybe moths. However, what holds true for an insect does not hold water for us. We have mental and physical control over our environment and thus, to some extent, over our destiny.

I expect that some individuals do not experience midlife crisis. Anything related to the turbulent years is not part of their behavioral patterns. Others supress any thoughts or feelings that do not appear normal to them. Many men, however, go through various degrees of hell during these trying years. Sometimes I see the same situation reflected in nature. During my treks in the mountains I have often seen a few trees survive the brutal forces of past avalanches. A few of them, though bent and twisted, continue to reach toward the light with their scarred branches. The majority of the trees are at the bottom of the slope lying in a mass of twisted trunks, roots, and branches.

Marriage/Personal Relationships

For thousands of men, midlife crisis begins with the breakdown of marriage and the family unit. What we see happening around us seems to be happening everywhere. Marriages are crumbling like mud huts during an earthquake. Once topics of separation and divorce were shocking bits of news and gossip. Today they are commonplace. When we hear the news that kings and princes are experiencing marital conflict, we usually do not raise our eyebrows but continue munching our sandwiches without missing a bite.

There are both positive and negative aspects related to the problem of whether or not to stay with a spouse. Life is short, and what is the point of living a life of pretending? Often you hear answers such as, "For the sake of my mother," or "For the sake of the children." How about for the sake of you? What do you feel? Are you playing a game with your feelings and thoughts? Is there any chance that at sixty years of age, when the road begins to narrow ahead of you, you will say, "Oh my God, what have I done?"

On the negative side, there is a fair amount of embarrassment associated with separation. At first, you do not want to reveal the news to your parents, let alone your friends, or your landlady. Maybe it reflects failure on your part as well as the onrush of grief, fear, guilt, regret, loneliness, and financial stress. For many of us it is truly midlife crisis with its accompanying pain.

Recently during a weekend in San Blas, Mexico, I met a man

in a crowded restaurant who was an explicit example of a man in menopause. Within five minutes, he was telling me about his personal problems. His wife was living with her boyfriend in their beautiful house. He was living in an apartment with a friend. He thought he still loved his wife but maybe he felt sorry for her, which was the reason he married her in the first place. He could not concentrate on his business so he decided to spend some time in Mexico to get away from the proximity of his problems. He owned a beautiful piece of property, an entire hilltop which overlooked the ocean. He talked about building a mansion there, and yet in every second sentence he referred to his problems. He was renting a house from a friend and thus required a few groceries. He said he hated shopping for Sani-Flush and soap because he had never done it in his life. Like many other men, he seemed terribly helpless in the store.

Later in the evening, he took me to a plush restaurant (maybe to pay me back for listening to him). With all his problems, George would look at every female who walked into the place. From the appearance of the crowd, it was quite obvious they were not living in trailers. In the middle of a sentence he would stop, and say, "John, what do you think about that one? Nice body, eh?" "George," I said, "she is young enough to be your daughter!" "Boy, I like them young!" he replied. He made comments to the waitress that were almost embarrassing. Poor George! He seemed to be emerging from a cocoon. His mind was going in all directions, but his overweight body sat in one place!

Two days later, when I returned to my Spanish lessons, I met Steve. Again, within five minutes he told me about leaving his problems behind in Chicago and wanting to learn Spanish so he could converse with the beautiful Mexican girls. He was thirty-six, in the process of ending a messy divorce, and desperately seeking another female.

A beautiful girl walked into the room.

"Boy," Steve said, "wouldn't the group be shocked if they saw me back in Chicago with a chick like her on my arm?"

"But Steve, a girl is not an object you take home to show off to your friends. You have women and jewelry confused!" I said.

"Oh yeah, but I love beautiful women. I would love to go to bed with that one," he replied, eyeing the same girl with great relish.

"Steve, you wouldn't know what to do with her if you did," I chuckled.

Steve didn't like my words, but in fact I was right. He told me he wanted a real young girl, maybe sixteen, so that he could have some young, inexperienced person idolize him, love him, and be some sort of servant. She had to be a virgin; there were no "ifs" or "buts" in his statement. I looked at Steve, shook my head, and walked to class.

Nobody in the school liked Steve. When he talked to anyone it was always related to sex, virginity, sex, morality, and sex. The girls hated him because he said that Canadian and American girls had no morals. In order to look for a new wife, he had to go elsewhere. Later we heard that Steve was spending some time in jail on a manslaughter charge. I felt ill. I could see some innocent young girl falling for him, if only for the simple reason that she wanted to live in the States. And she wouldn't even know about his past. How sick!

Let us again turn to George for a few minutes. Unlike my reaction to Steve, I enjoyed the two days I spent with George. I especially liked his honesty. I think he enjoyed having someone to listen to him. He had the money and I had the time. He trusted me. Maybe I saw a part of me in his conversation. Whatever the reason, we did agree to get together again in the future. George truly represented the evils of midlife crisis. His conversation reflected a fair amount of grief. He did not accept his separation, and he spoke rather mournfully about his children. He repeated several times that he had to remember to send his youngest daughter a postcard. He mentioned that his wife was very negative about his actions.

"I could never do anything right," he said. "The last time we were in a restaurant, she told me I wasn't eating the grapes right. Well, how does one eat grapes anyway?"

"I really haven't thought about that one," I said. "I usually tear them off the stem, pop them in my mouth, then spit the seeds out."

"Boy, that sure doesn't sound right!" he replied.

This all sounds familiar. When we dislike a person, we begin to dislike almost every little thing that person does. Soon that individual becomes one big walking error in the eyes of the other.

There was fear in his words. George did not know what the future had in store for him. He didn't seem to know what to do next and wasn't certain if any decision was right. He was worried about living a life of his own or meeting the wrong person again. "I really don't know!" was repeated time and time again. The whole question of where to live, what to do, whom to do it with, and even the problem of looking after himself were words reflecting anxiety. I added that his fears were very realistic.

As we conversed further, George also talked about regretting some of the things he had said and done in the past.

"Maybe if I had been more careful about spending more time at home instead of always making money I would be happier now. I told my children I wanted them to have a good life. That meant having things that I never had when I was young. I wanted an expensive house and I bought my wife a fur coat. Maybe my priorities were in the wrong place. In fact, I know they were in the wrong place, because nobody is happy now." He added, "but I think I have learned something I might use in the future. You know it's so hard to make sure you don't mix up what you think, feel, and do. I guess one can't be too careful!"

Finally, George talked about guilt and loneliness. He looked at the young girls, yet I think he felt like a dirty old man He felt like he was still cheating on his wife. He was not living reality. George thought that maybe he was not manly and lacked the macho image necessary to make it with girls. But why is George unable to accept himself, instead of worrying about what other men are like? Why is being macho so important to men? Who are they trying to fool other than themselves? I hope that George can do what is meaningful and right for him, and forget about some make-believe image that others have created for him. All the world may be a stage but I hope it is not a continuous movie.

George was a lonely man. He enjoyed my company because it gave him a chance to talk to someone. For many lonely people, human contact is always welcome. There is fear in always being alone. And yet even in my presence, I felt the man was very much in his own world with his own silent company.

Uncertainty/Decision Making

Generally midlife crisis is marked by the repetition of questions such as "what's it all about?" During this period, men find themselves in transition. It is common to find some moving to new neighborhoods, other parts of the country, and even to foreign countries. Each man experiences a sense of emptiness. Often when problems arise, there is considerable difficulty in making decisions, and some individuals tend to postpone any decision they make. It seems as though they want to wean themselves very slowly so they can move from one situation to an unknown one.

The inability to make decisions is often an aspect of new love affairs. Some men are dating, some are searching for the pot of gold, some are going steady for the seventh time, some are living with another woman, while others are on the verge of remarrying. Even though the love affairs may not be totally satisfactory, they often seem better than no love at all, and men will hang on to some of the feeble heartstrings that are left dangling in front of them. Again, they experience guilt, because they are leaning on another, fear of the unknown, regret at having done what they are doing, and grief over the hurt feelings created.

If you remain in a state of indecision, you will probably find yourself slowly deteriorating mentally and physically. You may find yourself in a hospital with some strange virus even though you tell everyone you were never ill before. You cannot run, drink, smoke, engage in sporadic heavy eating, and hope to feel the same as you did when you were eighteen. I have seen men work all day, take one girl for a few drinks, come home, change, and take another out to dinner. You repeat this and soon you find bags under your eyes big enough to hold your golf clubs. The sadness often comes when you question if it is all really worth it. Remember, there is one small difference between a twenty-five and a thirty-five-year-old fool. The older you are, the more mistakes you are able to make, and the more you have to lose.

Fear of Death

Many men in menopause have a genuine fear of death. They are very much aware that death is imminent. At the crossroads of life, there is an awareness that life does not go on forever. There is a quick mental check of accomplishments, and another quick check of how much time is left for unfinished business. Usually one experiences increased heartbeat, perspiration on the brow, and knees that want to buckle under the weight above them.

Death hits home when you see a friend, a relative, or even an acquaintance die. I clearly remember a suicide and a fatal heart attack which happened to two men I knew very well. Not only was I shocked, but the events literally forced me to look at my own life and to reevaluate some of my goals and values, knowing very well that the same could happen to me. I think that if more men realized that they are not going to be around forever and that the world can easily survive without them, they would live more fully from day to day. The future is another world.

Portrait of a Middle-Aged Man

When I think of a man in midlife, I picture an individual with thin, hairy, white legs, a pot belly, and a few strands of hair plastered across a bald forehead, or a permanent wave to create an illusion of fullness to hide a receding hairline. He is a person who owns a nice car, three-piece suits, and expensive underwear. However, when he looks in the mirror, he sees a series of road maps.

Women are as important to this man as life itself. His eyes are constantly searching the crowds. He sees a blond and whispers run through his mind. "Hey, psst, would you like to join me on safari?" I know one man who neatly fits this category. He tells me he sleeps with two women in this city and with others he bumps into at other watering holes. He is very proud of his achievements and feels that he is in great demand. Sometimes he has to punch himself for saying the wrong thing to the wrong person. What a waste of energy!

And yet, I've talked to many women who tell me that going to bed with a man is not uppermost in their minds. Many men think that women and sex are synonymous. I know that a lot of women would prefer a little kindness and gentleness in the light rather than a sexual encounter in the dark. Conquest is more of a problem for men than it is for women. Men spend a great deal of time worrying about their sexual abilities. Everything from size to satisfaction dominates their thoughts, and yet they must remember it is the person that counts and not the performance. Obviously sex manuals are not the answer to many problems in this area.

Problems multiply when one man attempts to form a stable relationship with a woman. Often he has children of his own and the woman he falls for is probably raising her own family. Unfortunately, the children are caught in the middle. He has to spread his energy more thinly. Sometimes he opens his eyes and stares at the ceiling wondering what he is doing, let alone if he is doing the right thing. He asks himself how it all happened and feels like tearing his past into little shreds and casting them into the path of a hurricane.

Along with all the sexual encounters and associated personal problems, men are often faced with job difficulties. When their minds spin with personal problems they have trouble concentrating on their work. They often take out their frustrations on others and blame everyone else for their problems. Some men change professions, some start a clean slate, while others become true workaholics. They bury themselves in work as a perfect escape from their weary worlds. They achieve in terms of money or status, but often little in personal growth.

You can easily be the person devastated by all the trauma of midlife loneliness. The merry-go-around with women will probably lead to the sex therapist. The inability to see beyond your arm's length may lead you to a hypnotist. The indecision in your life may force you to seek help from counselors and psychiatrists. You can feel sorry for yourself, or you can take some positive action and reach for a richer life. I am a great believer that first you have to want to help yourself before you can have others help you. The more time you spend chasing dreams, the longer you will remain in crisis. If you never open your eyes to reality, you can be heading into a journey of disappointments and grief.

How to Approach Midlife Crisis

The first positive step you can take is to spend some time alone. In fact, I think this is the secret to growing up in other stages as well. How can you even dream of being alone when you have been camouflaging your male menopause with your sports cars and list of eligible women? From discos, movies, dinners, and clandestine weekends, how can you possibly shift into neutral and wake up staring at the wall alone? Your first impulse is to get out of the eerie silence and get going. That's the first scary part, that uncanny, haunting sense of peace. Along with the peace comes the incessant calm. You swear you are going mad, but you hang in and don't panic. You slowly begin to see your world in a new way. You are frightened. You are emerging from the pupa.

What do you see? You notice your life in transition. You smile, you remember how you once wanted to change the world. The fact remains there is no proof that we have truth in this world. You simply do the best you can not hoping for miracles. You must listen and be listened to as well. Disappointments and injustice around us must be taken into stride. You cannot dwell on them as they are not worth the chest pains or the nail biting.

You will experience stress and anxiety. This is no surprise when you face uncertainty day in, day out. One of the underlying causes of anxiety is the fact that you do not know who you really are. As you slowly become your own person you will find the level of stress subsiding. You realize more and more who you are as a person. You gain in flexibility and openness to change. Anxiety and stress can both be handled during midlife crisis. Like loneliness, they do not have to guide your life for years to come.

Another step in the right direction is to retreat to a place where you can be by yourself, and yet have help if you need it. Whether you choose a retreat or some private place, you want to pay special attention to yourself as a person. If you are overweight, it might be the time to diet. You can engage in some form of exercise, walking, running, or whatever you want. You will look and feel better, and exercise will help decrease your level of stress. Exercise can be done in a place where you can be alone if you want, make friends, and, more importantly, get in touch with reality and overcome the fear of peace and calm. You will feel at peace with the world when you discover that you do not have to impress or perform. Cultivate one close friend. Have a quiet dinner. Watch the world unfold before your eyes.

What is success? What is happiness? For me, it means peace of mind and being able to be myself. This is a start. Discover what it means to you. Note that you are not a truly lonely person. More and more you learn what life means to you. What is love? What is life? You grow and you learn.

Some Individual Cases

Let us examine some other individual situations which might be common to this life cycle. As one example, let us consider a couple who have been married for eighteen years. When they first started life together, they had very little in terms of material goods and money. Before they knew it, they had their first child, then their second child, and by mistake a third child. Because of the close succession of births, the mother was kept busy with the numerous, everyday chores. The father was busy at work and adjusting to family life. The years passed rather quickly. As the children went from kindergarten to elementary school, the mother gradually found herself alone at home. Initially the feeling was one of great relief. By having the children off her hands during the day, she could have more time to herself. Coffee sessions, phone calls, and a craft seemed to occupy her time quite well. Soon the children were in high school and there were added financial burdens, but the children continued to occupy most of the parents' energies. Before they knew it, both parents found themselves staring at each other across the kitchen table. Life seemed like one big deflated balloon. Emptiness reigned supreme as each partner added very little to the meager relationship that had existed. Soon nothing was left. Both had been lonely, isolated people before, but now they were truly lonely. Life seemed to have very little left to offer. The years had passed quickly and both parents felt cheated, as though something in their lives had been missing. Slowly they began to reconstruct their individual lives. The experience was painful and lonely.

Let us take another example. We see a couple whose three children are attending high school. The family is very cohesive; they are not held together by selfish, neurotic needs. Each member is dependent on the other, but at the same time they are also individuals. Each one has his own special interests and pursues them when time permits. The parents have always been very good friends; they are able to give to each other as well as to their children. They enjoy their relationship and do not take much for granted. They do not have any great plans when the children leave home, except perhaps a trip overseas. None of the family members experiences any long-term loneliness; each is an independent person. Mother is not looking for twenty things to do to occupy her time; she has her favorite hobbies, bowling, and close friends. Father not only enjoys his work, but also finds time to play tennis and ski with the family. One might well ask if there are any families of this description around us. I think there are and they are truly fortunate to be in such an enviable situation. Loneliness is not part of their company.

Then there is another situation which is very common in our society today. Let us call the man Don. He is thirty-eight years old, the father of two children and was divorced at age thirty-three. He has all the payments to meet at the end of each month, occupy himself with his work, maintain some emotional ties with his children, and look after his own needs as well. For Don, life does not appear to be all fun and games. If you ask him how he is doing, he would tell you he is having a blast. He simply cannot admit that he is experiencing loneliness; he appears defensive. Don seems to spend most of his free time on the phone lining up dates. To someone on the outside, it may seem funny to think of dates during midlife, especially when many of them are not long-lasting experiences After one or two meetings Don is on the make again. If you ask him why he does not maintain a relationship for a longer period of time, he tells you that all the women he meets are a bit weird and he has no time to straighten them out. He simply cannot admit that he is ever wrong. When things get a bit rough, Don has a few drinks, and his smoking becomes a little heavier. Will he stop and look at himself one day? At this point there is only a slight chance. He must experience growth within himself before he is able to experience some relationship that is meaningful. However, life is now a vicious circle. He is truly in midlife explosion.

Finally, let us take a look at Ron. He is forty-two, and single, holds two degrees, and owns his own house and a big car. If you ask him what is most important in his life, he would say his work and his little poodle, Alphonse. You would swear that the dog was a human being the way it is treated. It is always spoken to in subdued language, even when it has soiled the white rug. After all, its nervous system is rather delicate, and what more can Ron say except, "Alphonse honey, you know where you have to go when you have to go, don't you dear?" Ron does not think that he will marry, but if the right one comes along, he may consider the possibility of a relationship. She must be educated, wealthy, attractive, a nonsmoker, and a nondrinker. The thought of meeting such a person seems remote. Ron devotes a great deal of effort to his work. There are meetings to attend, and reports to write. When you are "over the hill", there is less energy for other thrills in life. He and his friends attend an occasional concert, play, or ballet. Most weekends are spent in cleaning the house and shopping. There are no dates. Ron is not having a midlife explosion; it is more like a midlife puff!

CYCLE V:
SETTLING DOWN
(AGES 44–50)

Take time to work—
it is the price of success.
Take time to think—
it is the source of power.
Take time to play—
it is the secret of perpetual youth.
Take time to read—
it is the foundation of wisdom.
Take time to be friendly—
it is the road to happiness.
Take time to dream—
it is hitching your wagon to a star.
Take time to love and be loved—
it is the privilege of the Gods.
Take time to look around—
the day is too short to be selfish.
Take time to laugh—
it is the music of the soul.

Old Irish Prayer

For many during this cycle, turbulence ceases and calmness returns. When you look around, you see a large number of people who seem to fit this pattern. They are enjoying some stability in their lives. The die has been cast and all the decisions that have been made have to be lived with. It was a long wait to see some of the dust finally settle, but it was well worth the effort.

Positive Aspects

Money is somewhat less important in this stage. After all, many of the material goods you really desired, such as a house, furs, and new cars, have been acquired. You can afford trips to Hawaii. The children are off your hands, and other than the usual babysitting for grandchildren or pets, your own work occupies your time. Many of your values may not coincide with those of your children, but you have to accept the fact of change in values and life styles. Once in a while you grumble that you made do without a dishwasher and there is no reason why they have to have everything. Grandchildren are a great joy. You can truly enjoy them because you are not responsible for their upbringing. You may comment on the discipline or on the type of lives they are leading, but you usually keep your mouth shut.

Who do you turn to? A spouse is now an asset; she is someone you can lean on. You turn to each other for joy and sympathy because you no longer have your parents to turn to. To me this is very important; it is a great emotional loss when both parents die. I think of the day when my parents will not be around and I instantly experience deep sadness. Just the thought of losing them makes me very aware what a lonely experience it is. Parents are a source of support all of their lives. Children are never completely removed from the minds of parents, no matter how old or successful either children or parents may be. One of the more tragic aspects of life is when children no longer recognize their parents as people. The thought makes me very angry.

Others, who through fate or choice are living alone, continue to work and lead as fulfilling a life as possible. Most men who have not married would probably avoid the chance, even if one thought the money and companionship would be welcome. The fear of people being set in their ways often leads one to avoid getting trapped with a partner. This is not true for men who are recovering from the midlife crisis. If they are able to reorganize their thoughts and their total existence, they will not avoid meeting women. This cycle allows for another chance at achieving peace and harmony in relationships. For many it is like a second birth. In fact, I think that from my own experience and from the observations of others, man hits a peak in his late forties in terms of sophistication, confidence, and overall maturity. I hope that for the majority this holds true for the future years as well.

Friends are important in this phase of life. Of course, they are always important, but in addition to their spouses, people turn to some of their well-established friends, however few they may be. There are get-togethers at the dinner table, where they discuss their grandchildren. They talk about plans for retirement, but the ideas evoke a certain amount of fear and apprehension. The thoughts of some men slip into higher gear. Some have fantasies related to young women. There appears to be the same final attempt to solve problems left over from childhood. It is as though they still have to prove they are macho with all the associated desires. Their hair may be gone, or what is left is rather grey. Their joints ache after a few flings on the dance floor. However, the eyes still function when necessary and they have energy.

There are other positive aspects related to this life cycle. The first that comes to mind is related to work. It is probably in this stage of life that man is in his prime and is as influential as he will ever be. I especially think of many in business or administrative positions who are at their peak. This does not mean that they did not function well at an earlier age. However, if there was any positive growth in the first part of life, the individual is now reaping some of the benefits. Living in itself has now given each individual some wisdom and some information about life in general. Power is riding high; energy is being spent to maintain at least the level of achievement that one is used to. Let's face it. If the person has not achieved success by now, he does not have too many chances left to prove himself unless he luckily happens to be in the right place at the right time. We must admit that the right connections also help. Individuals who know the right people are able to shorten the time span required to reach their goal.

Financial success is something that is outside my real world. I imagine that the person who is caught in the game of making a lot of money must spend at least part of his time in lonely existence. The hours spent in scheming, dreaming, and making crucial decisions must be truly lonely times. If the individual is working beyond his intellectual and emotional means, then the strain must add to the lonely experience. I sometimes wonder how people reach the positions they hold above and beyond the political games that they play. At times it must be very difficult for them to hide their loneliness, their fears, and their general insecurity. Somehow the years of experience shield them from some of the icy blasts which they encounter from time to time.

It is often said that behind every successful man there is a woman who carries her share of the load. I hate to think of this as one of the functions of women in our society. If there is truth in the statement, then there must be a lot of wasted female talent. When I look around at the people I know, I must admit that in most cases the women can run circles around the men. I am speaking of couples that I know. Maybe the females did not experience as many hardships, but whatever the reason, they take first prize in the emotional and social sphere. As the men squirm in their shoes, the women are self-confident. While the men try to impress, the women act in a natural, effortless manner. I have been unable to determine the reasons for the difference in behavior. Maybe part of the answer lies in the expectations and pressures of roles that women must live with. I wonder how so many women can put up with all the nonsense.

If a marriage lasted well into the forties, then there is a high probability that the relationship will continue. By now the pattern of living is well established; if the marriage is a good one, the couple will continue to flourish through the years. If the relationship was not ideal, both partners may accept the situation for what it is worth. There is a feeling that it is too late to do much about anything; two lonely hearts continue beating as one. Financial and physical security gives each person some reason to stick it out to the end.

Some Negative Features

On the negative side, in today's stressful world, there is a possibility that one partner will pass on and leave the other to mourn. These are times for grief and loneliness. The male probably suffers a great deal because of his inability to cope with everyday chores of basic survival. The female may be left with many responsibilities that she was not accustomed to doing in the past. In either case, if there is some immediate family then some of the loneliness is averted. If there is no one to turn to, then loneliness hits with full force.

In addition, neither the male nor the female win too many beauty contests during this stage of life. The years have taken their toll. One has to take more pills, rest more, and eat less. People spend millions in an attempt to restore their youth. I wonder why one cannot accept the fact that nature takes a very natural course. It is important to keep in good physical shape by exercising and eating proper food, but there is little need to lose sleep over two wrinkles that form around the eyes; they simply represent your sense of humor. Now that people can afford them, clothing does not look quite like it would if the person were in his twenties. In fact, I wish that some people would quit acting and pretending. This is a time to be yourself.

In general, this cycle of life should receive three stars. It is the calm before the storm, but there are clouds on the horizon, and the sun's rays are slanting at a lower angle now. The days seem shorter; the time seems to fly even faster than before. We are now moving into the last stretch of the journey.

CYCLE VI:
MELLOWING AND OLD AGE

The following story appeared in the *Los Angeles Times*.

"I'm So Lonely. . . . Will Someone Call Me?"

Last Sunday, Mrs. Jean Rosenstein sat down at a small table in her cramped, one-bedroom apartment and painfully put her thoughts on paper.

The arthritis in her fingers made the writing laborious.

"I'm so lonely I could die," she wrote. "So alone, I cannot write. My hands and fingers pain me, pain me. I see no human beings. My phone never rings . . .

"I'm so very old, so very lonely. I hear from no one . . . Way past 80 years. Should I die. Never had any kind of holidays, no kind. My birthday is this month.

"If you ever feel sure the world ended. I'm the only one on earth. How else can I feel? All alone. See no one. Hear no one talk. Oh, dear God, help me. Am of sound mind. So lonely, very, very much. I don't know what to do."

She put the letter in an oversized yellow envelope, stuffed in a dollar bill and six stamps, and mailed it to the Times.

"Will someone call me?" she pleaded. The dollar was to pay for the phone call. The stamps were to be used if anyone would write her.

A Times reporter phoned her Wednesday morning, and she broke into tears. He asked if he could come to visit.

"Oh, God bless you," she cried. "I just knew someone would call. I need to get dressed, to get fixed up."

In a city of nearly 3 million people, Mrs. Jean Rosenstein—age 81—has no one.

Her home is on the first floor of an old, two-story apartment building at 1344 W. 4th St., not far from the Harbor Freeway. It costs her $60 a month out of the $200 she gets from Social Security and an old age pension.

A foldup bed protrudes from double closet doors. Flowered drapes hang from one window, which looks out on the wall of the apartment house next door. A dark blue dress serves as a shade. There is a battered brown couch, a dresser, a chair, a table.

"If I had somebody to talk to, they can come here," she said. "I'd buy the food. The only person who talks to me is the man who cashes my check."

"The people here, they won't talk to you. They say, 'Pay your rent and go back to your room.' "

"I'm so thrilled when you called this morning. I get so frustrated, so anxious to talk to somebody, just somebody. I have no company, nobody comes in."

She wore a brown print dress and a pink sweater coat with small pearls. She was once a nurse at Cedars of Lebanon Hospital but retired many years ago and moved to Florida with her husband, now dead.

They had a son Joseph, a writer, an Army veteran—but he died in 1962 and is buried in a military cemetery in San Diego. She moved to California a year ago.

"I have a sister and a brother in Florida," she said, "but they don't pay any attention to me. They're all well-to-do and have their own homes and own cars. Even the 18-year-old girl has her own car."

Occasionally, Mrs. Rosenstein takes the bus downtown to shop for groceries and saves her small change to give to the young Spanish children who congregate in the neighborhood.

"I used to bring them candy," she said, "but now they would rather have the money."

Her sister-in-law in Florida sent her $5 this week, and Mrs. Rosenstein indicated she wanted to give it to the Red Cross "for those poor people in Pakistan. They're starving to death."

She reads the newspaper daily—and watches television.

"If you are alone, you die every day," she said. "I can't do anyone any good. I can't do myself any good. I'd like to meet people, and whatever they like, I'd like too. I just eat and sleep. Sometimes I just dread to see myself wake up in the morning."

"Isn't anyone else lonely like me? I haven't found anyone yet."

When I look at this phase of life I think of Frank Sinatra singing about being in the autumn of his years. Autumn to me immediately evokes a feeling of melancholy, and probably that is the reason why this phase of life is associated with loneliness. It may not be the same intense loneliness that some experienced when life fell apart in the later twenties or thirties. Nonetheless, the silent company does visit many of our older people, sometimes for short periods, but often for many, many years.

Recently, I heard a reporter interview people in a large city. He asked them what their thoughts were with regard to retiring and old age in general. Every person expressed some apprehension and fear about the prospect of growing old. They feared loneliness, the loss of a spouse, and being somewhat worthless after a lifetime of work and productivity. In fact, I am surprised when I see people around me who are anxious to retire at the age of fifty-five. I must be odd, because I would like to continue teaching when I am in my eighties, if I live that long. People probably fear this last phase of life because they are closer to death, and this in itself evokes fear. I have seen an old person cry when he was close to death, and yet I have also seen an old person want to die. These are truly lonely times.

My Personal Experience with the Elderly

I might be an exception from the general populace because I admire and enjoy old people. Maybe one reason for my attitude relates to memories of my grandparents. I remember my grandfather with his black bushy moustache and his thick dark hair. My strongest memory of him will always be his singing ability. Every Sunday he would sing part of the Gregorian chants in his deep, baritone voice. I remember my grandmother telling me stories while I lay in bed. How great it was to go out in the frosty night together and gaze in wonder at the northern lights. When my grandparents left this earth I felt a piece of my world fall apart.

I now feel the same closeness toward my parents that I felt as a child toward my grandparents. I love to take my father traveling. He is seventy-three and as alert as I am, which may reflect badly on me. Since I left home when I was fifteen, I hardly ever knew him. During the past three years we have traveled, laughed, and talked for hours on end. I will cherish the memories as long as I live. But mothers cannot always stay home and babysit the house. We have traveled to a few exotic places as well. As with my father, it is a time for quiet talk, laughter, and a few tears.

Even outside my family, I enjoy conversing with old people. A few days ago I sat in front of a store eating my big ice-cream cone. Since I was sitting in a national park, there were people coming and going during the half-hour I was there. An old couple parked their new vehicle in front of me, and as they entered the store, I made a remark about their brand-new camper. We exchanged a few comments. They mentioned they were from Miami but enjoyed getting away during the summer months. When the man came out of the store, he watched me attack my ice cream and decided to buy some for the two of them. During our conversation they mentioned they were in their seventies and loved traveling. I commented how lucky they were to be in good health, and we exchanged a few more laughs. As she got into the truck, I heard her say to her husband, "Wasn't that fun?"

When I was in graduate school, we lived in an apartment block next to a dear, old Scotswoman. She used to visit a friend who lived in our apartment block. When I saw her, I would always ask, how she was or simply say, "Hi there!" She insisted we use her patio whenever we wanted, and even help ourselves to lettuce from her little garden. Even though she had a married son with two children in the city, they usually came to visit only once a week. She was the greatest person! She actually cried when we left the city.

Problems of the Elderly

To many, the experience of visiting old people is nothing new. Certainly thousands of us associate with old people, yet many of our young people are quite alien to the older generation. Because of mobility and various circumstances, many young families are separated from their aged parents. How often does a ten-year-old visit his grandfather in a nursing home? Rather than help old people, I have seen adults fight over property even before the death of their parents. I have seen old folks give their old age pension checks to their sons so they could pay off their debts. Meanwhile, the old folks eat warmed soup for most of the week. I know an old couple who have thousands of dollars in the bank. Their plastic flowers on the table are covered with a plastic sheet. Their carpet is covered by dozens of homemade rugs. They have no family and friends and live very frugally; they are terribly lonely people. Sad, but true. Often the motto seems to be "What can the old folks do for us?" rather than "What can we do for the old folks?"

Not all the elderly are lonely, but neither did all old people experience Cycle III, "Questions, Questions." However, I think that old age has the potential for being a very lonely experience. This is the third and last time when many people can encounter intense loneliness. The other two lonely stages I discussed were in Cycles I and III, Leaving Home and Questions, Questions. Whereas in the other stages loneliness could pass, in this final, mellowing stage, loneliness can eat into the hearts of many old people, and last through their remaining years. We sometimes see a prize photograph of an old man, worn down by the stresses of life, staring into space. Classic or not, old people in our society pose a problem, but, unfortunately their children do not always care. The remaining family often does very little to better an old mother or father's physical and emotional state. For some, old people are the lost generation.

With the improvement of medical science, old people tend to live longer. This poses a problem for society because these people require a roof over their heads and food to survive. Because of their age, many require more medical attention as well as physical care. For the old person who has reasonably good mental and physical health, a house and sufficient money, his life is far from dreary. Even though some have lost their husbands or their wives, life for them continues on a fairly comfortable level. There are cruises, trips, shuffleboard, and cards to occupy their time. I have seen little old ladies with grayish-pink hair, slick pencilled eyebrows, and excessive make-up eyeing guys young enough to be their grandchildren. Not all old people are alike; a few are still able to look, wish, and sigh.

As many as three-quarters of our old people own their own homes, but only about two-thirds are living in the communities where they spent most of their lives. Up to a third of our old people live at or near the poverty line. Only an old age pension and other small monthly checks keep them alive. Some live in rooms that aren't fit for dogs. I feel that the old folk in rural areas are better off than their city counterparts. Farmers often return to the town where they shopped, talked to their friends, and attended both happy and sad events. Many do not worry about cars because they are able to walk to the shops for their groceries. In fact, some make several trips a day just for something to do. It is a good feeling to experience a sense of belonging. The entire community is very familiar to them, and what could be boring to a young person is more than adequate for the aged. In addition, there are always large gardens to look after all summer long.

Compared with rural people, city dwellers do not have the same community feeling. Friends are more difficult to meet because of distance and traffic, and many live in small apartments or small rooms. People seem to rush along the sidewalks and not everybody smiles and says hello. In fact, often young people will not give up a seat on the bus for the elderly who get pushed around and sometimes laughed at. Who said that retirement and old age are fun? The problems of everyday existence can further lead to alienation and loneliness. Unfortunately, money is a problem as it often is in all life stages. An abundance of money does not solve loneliness, but a lack of it can seriously affect happiness and contentment.

Living in poverty is no challenge; in fact, it is a mere existence where survival is the key. Cheap, walk-up apartments, a scarcity of material goods, and improper food can quickly lead to despair and heartache. Add a few physical and emotional ills, and you soon have a classic case of survival. No, happiness does not abound in these situations. Nights become long journeys into days.

On the other hand, we do not necessarily have to assume that wealth will lead to happiness, fun, and a fairy tale existence. Loneliness does not escape the wealthy group of old people. Having the financial means, many of these people retire to more expensive housing, to retirement communities with guards, fences, and all the facilities for a good life. Life is spiced with travel and so-called comraderie. Quite often one is fooled by the facade because, to me, these are the places for some of the very lonely people we are talking about. If a new house, a pool, and a golf club membership do not make younger people happy, then it does not follow that old people will be better off with them. The idea of retirement areas does benefit the developers, but I feel what old people need are their friends and familiar surroundings. Friends are hard to come by, and it seems the older you get, the more difficult it is to make close ties. When you are in your seventies, the idea of forming close relationships in a retirement area seems almost impossible. People get together to chat but they usually talk about their children, which can be boring if you do not know them. Many talk about their aches and pains, but why listen when you have your own? On the surface it appears like a happy arrangement, but underneath the smiles are many sad faces. Travel can be tiring as well. You can expect to get exhausted when you are hauled around by bus for ten hours a day. Even the food has to be fortified with pills. Often the most exciting event on these tours is bedtime.

In all cases, inflation hits the elderly more than other segments of the population. People who saved all their lives find their dollar eroding year after year. With the price of utilities, food, and clothing on the rise, the dollar has to stretch more than ever before. I was reminded of this the other day when I watched an old woman at a supermarket checkout counter. She was buying one tomato, two small bananas, and about fifteen cherries, and paid a sum that would have purchased twice as much the year before.

Nursing Homes, Family Ties

More than anything, our old people suffer from loneliness and alienation as a result of weak family ties. This is not just an accident. People move around in search of work and promotions, and the net result is loss of close contact with their parents. Even though children do make the occasional phone call, old people would prefer physical contact. What can you do if you live three thousand miles away? You have enough of your own problems with children, bills, and salary demands. Visiting grandma and grandpa looks terrific on television but in reality is quite different. Besides, if the old folks can't get around too well and children find little time for them, there is always the nursing home to look after their survival needs. Why should young adults worry?

Nursing homes have developed as a necessary social institution in our society. If they did not exist in our country, many old people would lie around helpless like some of the elderly one sees in India. Some of the homes are better than others but are never like your own four walls. It takes a fantastic person to react to the lame and feeble with love and care. However, I think that if children do not have a warm feeling toward their parents, how can you expect a stranger to respond with love? Certainly many do and more power to them, but for some it is only a job. Probably up to one-half of the people in nursing homes never see their children; they appear to be forgotten in the rush. But, some of these people hope for a happier, less lonely existence. What solutions can we offer? Is there any possibility for making life any easier for the aged? Is loneliness a necessary part of their lives, or can the condition be avoided? What has happened to our feelings? How can we forget people who nursed our fevers through long, lonely nights?

How the Elderly Can Cope

One of the most important attributes at any age is health. People must prepare for old age not only in terms of bank accounts and property but also in terms of preserving their health. When I look around and see so many women twice their normal size and men with bellies hanging over their belts, I begin to wonder. One must eat properly and exercise faithfully. This does not mean you will end up being Tarzan at eighty. However, if you are able to walk when you are forty, fifty, and sixty, then you will probably enjoy walking at seventy. I have seen people in their seventies hiking in the mountains. How happy I am for them!

You do not get exercise when you join your friends and watch all the soap operas on television. If your feet can carry you, then use them when you have the opportunity. It is true that many of the elderly did not have the opportunity to enjoy some of the sports that younger people can enjoy today. For example, if you were able to ski when you were young, then there is a better chance that you will be able to ski when you are seventy. It is next to impossible to start a new sport when you are old. The same holds true for travel. If you traveled when you were younger, then you will enjoy a few trips in later years. I greatly admire the person who can travel the world with a knapsack at the age of sixty-eight! I wonder about the many people who still have their health and money but sit around and do very little. With any physical activity, you must listen to your body. If it tells you that you need a rest, then take a nap or at least lie down for an hour. Remember that you do not have to prove to others what you can do; you have already done that in your lifetime.

Your mental state has an incredible effect on your everyday life. Your mind is like a muscle. If you use it then it will serve you well, but if you let it rest then it becomes weak and does not function at a high level. Do not let your brain stagnate by watching hours of television. Read a paper, a book, a magazine, and listen to the daily news. You should try to be involved with the world and with your environment. Try to think young; where possible, have some younger people to associate with. Remember that a change is as good as a rest.

It seems a farce that a person should retire at age sixty-five. Some people could work until they are eighty or more. We seem to have some funny ideas about age and retirement. Why is sixty-five a magic age? Why not fifty-five or sixty? To leave work and feel useless is a human tragedy. If a person has his mental and physical health, he should continue to work and contribute to society if he wishes.

If you have talents, use them. I am surprised that schools and universities do not think of asking any of the hundreds of retired professors to contribute to discussions and lectures. I look upon most individuals in their seventies as a storehouse of information. For example, teachers in my neighborhood discuss early settlements with their fourth graders. Why don't they invite some of the original pioneers who can provide more information to the children than any film strip or movie? I feel certain that the young children and the pioneers would enjoy the interaction very much.

Do not feel useless or a burden to society. You have already contributed most of your life to your family and your work. Do not live for your family alone; they can probably do well without your help. I have seen some old parents spending a great deal of their time and money helping a son buy a business, a farm, or a car. There is no reason why you should be wearing your son's old suit that was worn twenty years ago. This is not the time to wear discarded clothes. You will feel much better in something new for a change. During this stage in life you can afford to be a little selfish! I recently spent a few minutes conversing with a sixty-six-year-old woman who was vacationing in one of the plush hotels in the Canadian Rockies. She was truly enjoying herself as much as the interesting Australian who sat next to her. She said that she did not get along too well with her children. There was a twinkle in her eye when she made the remark. I think what she meant by that statement was the disappointment her children expressed because she was not spending money on them but rather on herself. Remember that you are still the most important person around and you must take care of yourself with tender, loving care.

I suggest that people maintain their friendships; friends are as important as money when you grow older. The closer one retires to where his friends live, the better off he is; the environment is not as strange as it could be otherwise. To move to a beautiful housing development in the sun, thousands of miles away from friends is not always the wisest thing to do. Such a move would appeal only to certain individuals who have always been self-sufficient. I can understand why some people prefer the cold prairie winters to balmy Mexican weather. The warmth on the outside may not necessarily spread to the inside!

I wish more families would provide for their parents. I cannot imagine my parents being stuck in an old age home. They have done so much for me; I would never turn them away. How wonderful to see the woman across the street in her eighties doing some of the cleaning and cooking in the household. Her daughter, son-in-law, and the children go to college while she stays home. Everybody wins in this situation. Why can't we see more of this in our society? Homes are big enough to house half a community, and yet individuals feel there is not enough privacy. We were looked after for years and years so why can't we reciprocate? Oh sure, I know we are busy and don't always get along with our parents. We are so lucky to have quick solutions. Most often we don't even try; usually we are more interested in what father can do for us. Certainly it does become a problem when we have people who are bedridden or crippled, since we are not equipped for total care. As I see it, today we are so self-centered, so wrapped up in our own world, we forget to care for our own parents.

In the meantime, thousands continue to lead lonely lives in the absence of any human warmth. Only death finally gives them relief from existence. Is this what years of struggling are all about? If someone were to ask me what the best thing is for our old people, I would reply that personal contact and affection from their families is the answer. There is no reason why they should suffer any loss of respect. The majority of old people truly love to see their grandchildren. If there is strife and the children are not allowed to see their grandparents, the pain is deep and silent. If a child does not have any relationship with a grandparent, he suffers as well. There is something very beautiful when the young and the old are together. Let us give our old people the most that we can give. I am not thinking of alarm clock radios and carpets, but of love and all the caring feelings that we are capable of sharing.

And so we come to the end of a long journey. What happens from birth to the end can fill several volumes. Regardless of who you are, you still have some control over your life. How you sleep in your bed will depend on how you make it. Some of you travel a rather smooth journey, with very little loneliness and sadness. For others, the trip is a journey through hell. You cannot always talk about fate or luck. You must look at yourself and pause in your busy world to see what is happening to you. You are your own best friend. Do not let yourself down. After all, who can replace someone as unique as you are?

six
Loneliness: What We Feel and Experience

A few years ago I was in a coffee lounge discussing human problems with a few of my colleagues. I had finished reading *Loneliness* by Clark Moustakas; this book deals with a subject that has not been widely written about. I was impressed with the book because someone had finally written about a problem that I felt touches many of us. Furthermore, Moustakas discussed positive and negative aspects of loneliness. I never thought that loneliness, with its accompanying pain, could ever hold anything positive for me. When I mentioned some aspects of loneliness to one member of the group, whom I considered the loneliest person in the entire building, he quickly remarked that he was never lonely and the subject was not worth the energy needed for discussion. I sat back, somewhat dazed by his remark. Questions ran through my mind. Is it a sin to admit that we are lonely? Is loneliness some dreaded incurable disease? Is it ever possible to see ourselves as we appear to others? There was no further discussion, but the subject of loneliness remained among my thoughts through the years.

I recall watching Roy Bonisteel's "Man Alive" series on television. I was greatly moved by his interest in and concern with loneliness in our society. Mr. Bonisteel interviewed several people who were willing to discuss loneliness and how it affected their lives. They talked about the haunting feeling associated with loneliness, as well as their attempts to alleviate at least some of the suffering associated with the silent company. I discovered that the subject was not taboo for everyone.

As the months passed, I noticed a few articles in various magazines dealing with loneliness, but nowhere could I read a detailed account of the subject. I discussed it with close friends. I observed the behavior of others. Questions filled my thoughts. "What are the reasons underlying man's lonely existence?" "What behavior do people exhibit when they are lonely?" How often we hide our feelings behind our loud laughs, our endless conversations, and our brilliant use of words! Behind our facade, we often feel so very lonely. We humans, who are such unique creatures, are often so dismally alone and lonely.

Some people are truly lonely but they are usually not fully aware of their state. They live from day to day what to them appears to be a normal life. However, what may appear to be a lonely life for one may not be viewed as such by another. Then there are individuals who deny their loneliness. They are afraid to reveal their feelings to others. To them, loneliness is like some dreaded plague and only fate can explain why they are its unfortunate victims. Finally, there are a few healthy people who are not afraid to discuss their loneliness with friends and acquaintances. They are concerned with taking appropriate action to improve their lives.

As a society we love to use labels. We observe individuals and classify them as lazy, bright, slow, shy, crazy, or dozens of other adjectives. Labels are a form of diagnosis; once we are able to put a person into a certain slot, we feel that part of his problem is solved. We label other people as being lonely, but do we ever apply the term to ourselves? The truth of the matter is that we often enjoy diagnosing other people, but seldom look at ourselves. We enjoy giving advice to others but often shrug the idea of accepting other people's advice. We should do our own homework before we counsel others.

Loneliness is a universal concept; the term has a fairly common meaning. Wherever I may be, if a person tells me he is leading a lonely life, I think I understand what he is saying. Regardless of the circumstances, he is experiencing something that is very similar to what I experience when I am lonely. Loneliness seems to be a common thread that is woven into societies.

As human beings, we are very similar in terms of what we require in order to survive. Obviously, loneliness is something that most of us do not need. However, one mistake we make is that we tend to look beyond ourselves for explanations, reasons, and remedies. When we think of loneliness, we immediately think of relationships. We visualize some poor soul who lives alone and has very few people with whom to share human warmth. I do not think this perception is accurate. I have known individuals in the company of others who I felt were very lonely people. Is this some form of contradiction? Not necessarily. Relationships are only one aspect of loneliness. The other aspect is we as individuals, as humans in the midst of millions. This means I must first focus on myself rather than on others. Instead of blaming others for my lonely existence, I must focus on myself as a unique individual. However, we often fear looking at ourselves, and admitting to a frightening label such as loneliness. It is no easy task to put one's house in order, and yet I firmly believe that this is where the journey begins, a journey that can lead to a more fulfilling life.

LONELINESS: A DEFINITION

Defining loneliness is like trying to define love, because we know when it is present and when it is gone, but we have limited words to describe the total feeling. I think that we do not require a clear definition of the concept since most of us have experienced loneliness and know what we are discussing. It is possible that a few people have never experienced loneliness; they would probably constitute a minority. On the other hand, one may be extremely lonely but completely deny the feeling to himself and to others.

Loneliness relates to feeling. Since we tend to do strange things with feelings, loneliness may not be perceived very objectively. Loneliness is an awareness of being in a unique, isolated state. The sensation is intense, sharp, and all-encompassing; it embodies moments of pain, despair, disillusionment, and rejection.

Loneliness produces feelings of bleakness, desolation, and sadness. The experience can be compared to an endless, solitary journey through space. There is a feeling of being cut off from all human warmth, a feeling that no one cares.

The body responds to these feelings with certain side effects. The individual feels empty inside. Facial expressions become impassive. One feels tired, as if a heavy burden had been placed on his shoulders. The lonely person may also experience some fear and anger. Being cut off from direct human relationships, the person turns inward. Instead of verbal interaction, he spends more time dwelling on his own thoughts. When the feelings become extreme, the individual may slip into a state of depression.

One must look at loneliness more closely. Even though it is experienced by thousands of people, the degree of loneliness is not necessarily the same. I have observed people's behavior when they were alone, in one-to-one interaction and in groups. I have thought about my own behavior and attempted to give some rational reasons as to why I behaved the way I did in certain situations and how I felt about my actions. I have observed that some people feel good about themselves. They appear confident, at ease, and hold their heads just a bit straighter and taller than some others. True, there is often a thin line between holding one's head high and holding it too high. To feel overconfident can be as disastrous as being a coward. Overconfidence can cover up emptiness and weakness.

Individuals who have self-esteem and confidence are fortunate. They can go for long walks, travel alone to Europe, or live on their own in an apartment without feeling totally lonely. I have seen people in relationships in which their confidence was torn to shreds by their partner's behavior. They were never given praise, and they felt worthless as human beings. In general, they felt somewhat empty and useless as individuals and partners in the relationship. Thus I think one aspect of loneliness precedes the world of relationships. It begins with ourselves.

Loneliness I, II, and III

Even though loneliness has both emotional and social components, I wish to analyze its origin. We immediately think of relationships. But why can two people who live together be the loneliest people in the world? After all, they do have each other. One must examine the quality of that relationship because the presence of one person may do very little for the welfare of another. But what does quality refer to? It refers to you as an individual and who you are as a human being. Thus the basic source of loneliness originates with each human being. I call this Loneliness I. If you do not feel good about yourself, if you feel worthless and have little self-confidence, then you are a lonely person. How can I be happy in a relationship? How can I like others when I do not like myself? How can I be happy with others when I am not happy being with myself? The focus in Loneliness I is on the self. You must truly enjoy your own company. You are your own best friend. This seems so basic. After all, when we feel different from others because we are fat, skinny, ugly, or brilliant, we are in fact experiencing Loneliness I. Conquering it means we can progress, but not necessarily free ourselves from all loneliness. Why is this the case?

We human beings need other people; we cannot live in total isolation. Yet loneliness can penetrate our relationships. I refer to the loneliness associated with the lack of meaningful relationships as Loneliness II. When people talk about loneliness, they are most often referring to Loneliness II; however, I think that the majority of people are at the level of Loneliness I, and because they are unable to establish significant relationships, they also experience Loneliness II. Loneliness I and II combine to form Loneliness III or *total loneliness*. In this text, I use the term *loneliness* to refer to Loneliness III. Many people are hoping to conquer Loneliness I and neglect Loneliness II. This is obviously an individual choice; one can see why some people are happy to live alone and in fact lead a richer life than others involved in a relationship. Whether such a person is leading a full life is another question. In short, the experience of Loneliness I plus Loneliness II may be more traumatic than experiencing only Loneliness II. Do we simply accept our fate and make the best of life? Certainly not. We will later learn how we can help ourselves to overcome total loneliness; it is within our reach.

Thus, there are two conditions that lead to total loneliness. The first is a lack of love for the self and the second, the inability to establish meaningful relationships with others. The two conditions exist in a hierarchy. The first level, love for self, must be met before one can move to the second level, the establishment of relationships.

Overcoming Loneliness I:
Self-Love

As a unique human being, you must truly like yourself. You must feel that you would rather be with yourself than with anybody else in the entire world. This feeling must underly your behavior. You must feel confident about yourself. It is not necessary to be president of a company or drive a Rolls Royce to feel great. A street sweeper can feel good about himself. External status does not necessarily lead to a greater love for self. By "self," I mean your uniqueness, your total awareness of yourself. Your self-concept is your self-image, which is a combination of what you think of yourself as well as what others think of you. This total picture is one of the biggest motivators of your behavior.

So many good things happen when you discover you are your own unique companion, someone you can truly enjoy. You must honestly care about yourself and feel you are a worthy person instead of always putting yourself down, feeling guilty and worthless. Furthermore, if you do not like yourself you will be jealous of people around you. You will feel they are better looking or more sexy, or they do more things with their lives than you do. You do not want jealousy to accompany loneliness.

It has been said that self-knowledge is necessary in order to enjoy the good life. Of course, this is easier said than done because I think many people are usually afraid to look into their souls. However, it is necessary from time to time to do some honest self-evaluation. It is not easy to assess who you are as a person. Feeling worthless can be as damaging as feeling omnipotent. Honest acceptance of what you truly feel about yourself is one of the more difficult tasks in life. Often it is necessary to rely on information from others; this can give you a more total picture of yourself. But are people always honest with us? On the basis of your perceptions and the perceptions of others, you must decide who you are as a person. You can proceed along the roads of life by conquering the basic level of Loneliness I.

Overcoming Loneliness II:
Communication

Once we have achieved healthy self-love, we can move to the next level by conquering Loneliness II. We have learned to live with ourselves, and this ability enables us to move to the second level. We must go beyond self and reach out to others. We have established a firm base from which we can move out and risk. The important aspect of reaching out is to search for a friend, a person with whom we can share our feelings with honesty and depth. This individual cannot be a casual acquaintance. Whether or not we live with that person is not the determining factor. What counts is who he is as a person. Friendships do not come easily; they require a great deal of love and work. The level of involvement will be reflected in our ability to cope with ourselves. The more complete we are, the deeper our relationships will be. Meaningful relationships require commitment and growth. They are not casual encounters.

Relationships are not confined to people. It is possible to relate to many aspects of nature such as a sunset or a beautiful flower. A graceful animal can be an object of inspiration. Some people relate to pets better than they do to humans. Whether this is good or bad is debatable. Certainly there are some elements present in human relationships that are absent in other relationships. Hugging a tree may not be a rewarding experience for many.

When you are able to reach out to others, you have mastered Loneliness I. However, it is still possible to temporarily experience Loneliness II. Regardless of what you do, you will at times find yourself temporarily estranged. A weekend meeting where you are removed from the family can be a very lonely experience. Likewise, a hospitalized person may also experience many lonely hours. In general, people who are away from their loved ones for a short period of time will experience intense loneliness.

There are many variations of Loneliness II. The time spent in making a decision can be extremely lonely. Death, illness, or separation usually lead to intense degrees of Loneliness II. The majority of administrative positions are often accompanied by many lonely hours. What the individual gains from power and prestige he sacrifices to loneliness. The general detachment required in the decision-making process compounds the total situation. One can shift between Loneliness I and Loneliness II, where the difference is mainly of time, intensity, and focus. Even though Loneliness I usually lasts for a longer period of time, Loneliness II can be more intense. The strength and depth of a relationship influence the intensity of a lonely experience. Where one person experiences severe loneliness over a number of days, others will experience the loneliness for weeks, months, and even years. In extreme cases, some individuals use their lonely state as a crutch. It gives them something to cry and complain about to others. Feeling sorry for yourself is as disastrous as feeling sorry for others, since mere pity does not change the situation.

One might note another interesting phenomenon which will be discussed in more detail later. Loneliness per se is usually not the biggest problem one has to deal with. It is what a person does with the loneliness that matters. Many people have difficulty coping with loneliness because they are afraid to admit to themselves and others what they feel. Some individuals attempt to flee loneliness by trying to be terribly busy, by laughing and talking a lot, or by sleeping their lives away. People will go to great extremes in the attempt to run away or hide from loneliness. We become fantastic psychological acrobats by playing with our emotions as well as the emotions of others. The whole operation may be a defense mechanism. Because we are vulnerable, it is necessary to protect ourselves. We have faster planes and cars but we still cannot run away from ourselves. For many, this is a sad truth.

FEAR OF LONELINESS

Because man fears loneliness, he often spends hours worrying about his fate. We are all made to believe that as males and females we must naturally find a mate, eventually settle down in a cute little bungalow, and raise a family. We must agree that there is joy in good relationships. However, the ideal mate does not always come along at the right time. Some become afraid at the thought of spending the rest of their lives with an aging parent or by themselves. Such individuals sometimes jump into relationships at the earliest opportunity. This may not be a wise thing to do. Yet there is fear in being alone and lonely. Also, fear of loneliness keeps some people in their present state of existence. Fear of the unknown prevents them from moving into new environments and new relationships.

Marriage is often sought as a solution to the fear of loneliness. Many people probably think the married person is free from loneliness, and the person living alone is to be pitied. How can you think of a person being lonely if he is surrounded by a family? However, a person can be terribly lonely living with another person; for some people, an object can be better company than a human being. Simply being with another person is not a cure for loneliness. The quality of the relationship you have with that person is the significant factor.

An individual in our society can be compared to someone adrift on a body of salt water. There is a great need for water but the person is unable to quench his thirst. You think that by merging in the crowds, by being in the middle of the masses, your need for companionship will be satisfied. However, the chance of quenching your lonely feeling is probably as remote as your ability to climb Mount Everest in sneakers. Loneliness continues to linger and haunt your life like some dark shadow.

Another interesting phenomenon is that we fear total quiet or total isolation, even when we truly need it. How many people keep their television on just for the noise? Some have the radio competing with the television at the same time. There is something about silence that is frightening, probably because of its association with stillness and even lifelessness. We tend to avoid it. But how inviting silence can be! How wonderful it is to be by ourselves with quietness engulfing and immersing us. I remember some of the truly quiet moments I have experienced while hiking. What a unique experience to stand in a forest in total silence, without a single leaf stirring! This is an experience as unique as life itself. Ironically, in our civilization, we are often unable to spend too much time on our own. And yet we need some isolation to discover who we really are.

Recently, one of my students told me about her experience in a restaurant. She decided to treat herself to a dinner in a classy restaurant. Having spent a few hectic days she wanted some peace and quiet, to be by herself, and enjoy a few moments with her thoughts. Did she get the chance? Of course not! She was bombarded by offers from the waiter, as well as from other men who sat around her. She said her stomach was upset long before the dessert appeared on the table. Why can't others respect one's desire for a little peace, solitude, and reflection?

A problem develops when the fear of loneliness is not dealt with. In *Loneliness and Love* Moustakas feels that fear of loneliness is a sickness which promotes dehumanization and insensitivity among humans. This is a serious problem. Alienation is an unhappy aspect of modern society. However, when man is alienated from his own self, when he is alienated from his own feelings, insensitive to his own grief and to his own fear of experiencing loneliness, the problem becomes more serious. How can he share the pain, loneliness, and misery of other people, if he cannot experience it in himself?

There is merit in experiencing some loneliness as well as the fear of this loneliness, and our attitude may benefit from the ordeal. We usually think of loneliness from a very negative point of view, but this may be the wrong approach. The experience can make us more perceptive and aware of our feelings and our sensitivity to others. Denying our feelings does not enable us to perceive reality as it is; it does not enable us to see ourselves as we are. Loneliness can be positive if it lets us experience our feelings in depth, think constructively, and plan action. The experience can lead to positive growth. If a person is forever running away from his loneliness, his fears do not diminish. Fear is a natural emotion; however, coping with the fear takes strength, courage, and honesty.

ALONENESS AND LONELINESS

It is necessary to understand that living alone does not necessarily lead to a lonely existence. What is the major difference? The individual who is alone may not experience the detachment from others which creates the feeling of Loneliness II. This person may be able to find time to think and to plan. The relational deficit may exist, but he does not experience living in an isolated environment. How can this happen?

Being alone and loneliness can be best explained in terms of

Loneliness I and Loneliness II. First, take the case of Mr. Smith. He is twenty-eight years old, a school teacher who lives alone. When asked if he is lonely, his reply is negative. You look at Mr. Smith more closely. You notice that he has a very positive self-concept. He feels good about himself. He does his work well, he has confidence and speaks in a positive way. You can almost envy his happiness. Because he enjoys being with himself, and does not fear his emotions, he can also reach out. He has two very close friends. Some people would say he has the best of both worlds. He can be alone, and he can also be with others. Mr. Smith may secretly be the envy of many of his colleagues. Loneliness is not part of his life.

Here is another example of a man living alone. Mr. Trap has lived in a one-room log cabin in northern British Columbia for thirty-two years. The obvious question is how can he bear the total isolation? How can he possibly relate to the stars, wind, or clouds? How can he be happy if he is deprived of human relationships? Mr. Trap truly enjoys being by himself. He does not experience Loneliness I. Sometimes it is difficult to imagine another person relating to a tree or a bird in a manner that is more satisfying than relating to a human being, but I can understand this. I recall camping with a friend deep in the wilds of the Rockies. One morning a bird joined us for breakfast. He hopped around our campsite for more than an hour and shared our breakfast. He would tilt his head and stare at me for minutes at a time. When we left the campsite, the bird followed us until we entered a dense forest. How quickly I became attached to him, and how sad I felt about leaving him behind.

One might argue that relating to nature does not have the depth that human relationships have. There may be some truth to this statement. Since people are able to interact verbally, they often rely on feedback and intimacy that can never compare to the relationship one may have with, say, a pet bird. On the other hand, there are many occasions when I feel ecstatic while looking at a beautiful sunrise. Thus, I can envision Mr. Trap living alone and feeling less lonely than many of his species piled up in high-rise apartments.

On the other hand, take the case of Mr. Tutt. He also lives alone in a small one-room cabin and earns his living by trapping. When you look at him, your soul shivers. He looks downright scary.

He left civilization years ago because of his distrust for man. He regards trees as something to walk around or use for firewood. Snow is useful only for locating animal tracks. There is little joy in seeing the sparkle of flakes in the slanting rays of sunlight. Inside Mr. Tutt is an angry man and derives little enjoyment from living. He is truly alone and lonely. His life is merely existence.

There are no two people who experience aloneness in the same manner. The basic variables of the situation are never the same. One factor that should be mentioned, in addition to self-concept, relationships, and temporary conditions, is age. The majority of people in their twenties are extremely mobile; they seem to be on the go all the time, spending many hours at work, with friends, or at sources of entertainment. On the other hand, a person in his sixties or seventies is less mobile. He spends a great deal of time alone, living in the past. Often there may be a great deal of heartache when such a person is thrust into a different environment. Old friends are left behind, and if there is no immediate family to live with, there is no choice but to live alone.

Of course, aloneness can be accompanied by Loneliness I and II. Take, for example, the executive who is on a business trip, alone in his hotel room. One week ago, his wife packed her bags and left for London. When he discovered this, he was visibly shaken. He felt rejected, he thought of himself as a failure, and felt anger surge through his body. Regardless of how he perceived the relationship, he now fears the future. He often borders on depression. As he sits in his hotel room staring at the television, loneliness shares his company.

Why might one person be temporarily alone and feel very little loneliness? He is aware that being alone is only a temporary state, and that even if there is some feeling of loneliness, it is never intense. He can sit back and think of the relationship he has. He is aware that there is someone who really cares for him as a person, one who thinks of him in the same way that he thinks of that person. It really does not matter who the person is, because the important factor is the relationship he has with that person. He feels good about himself and his relationship as well. He can cope with the aloneness. As he looks at the lights of the city below him, the phone rings. He answers and a smile spreads across his face.

Let us examine another situation. A few months ago, I met a man who had left his home in Latvia, USSR. He was not too excited about leaving, but his son had left for Israel and wanted his father to join him. The family had emigrated to Israel, but after several months decided that it was not the ideal country in which to start a new life. Apparently the problems of language, low salaries, and climate forced them to move on. Unsettled, they came to Canada to seek a new life. When I was introduced to the sixty-seven-year-old man, he was living alone in a high-rise apartment. I was very impressed with his warmth and honesty. His son, daughter-in-law, and grandson were the only living relatives in the city, but like many families, they did not live together as an extended family. Was he happy? No, he was not pleased with his existence here. He had a job in a warehouse, but nobody really bothered with him at work, and his son phoned him only once or twice a week. He spent hours in his apartment or took long walks. As I conversed with the man, I felt great empathy. He had medals from the war, pictures, books, and other mementos; he seemed to live only in the past.

"I feel so alone and lonely here," he said. "Nobody really cares if I exist or not. Look, I could die here and nobody would know for a couple of days probably. When I was in the old country, people knew me. They always said hello and asked how I felt. Never a day went by without somebody checking my place if they did not see me around. Here I feel useless. I really miss my friends. I wish I hadn't left, but it's too late to go back."

About four months later, he died. Certainly one cannot attribute his death to being alone and lonely. However, I felt that loneliness did contribute to his untimely death. One might also add that this example illustrates the importance of having true friends.

During the past few years, the thought of doing your own thing has become more acceptable so that there is less questioning as to why a person chooses a different life style. However, people continue to assume that being alone is abnormal, undesirable, or indicative of a problem. Have you ever been in the company of a loud person when you were in a quiet mood and wanted to be alone? Have you ever been in a car with some other person when you were in no mood to talk? The other person does the talking for both of you. You stare at the person, but he keeps on talking. If you do not respond, the assumption is that something is bugging you, that there is something definitely wrong. We somehow assume that it is not our nature to engage in unusual forms of behavior such as quietness. If you do not respond, then I assume that you are angry at me. Don't we feel sorry for some poor creature traveling in a car by himself? We automatically think that something is wrong because it is just not natural for a person to be by himself. A holiday is not a holiday when you have only your poor little self for company.

POSITIVE ASPECTS OF SOLITUDE

Rather than looking for peace and solitude, something which is so precious in our society, we often tend to avoid it. Solitude is beautiful. It is a time when we do not have to respond to others. It is a time when we can forget about all the challenges and intellectual stimulation that we receive from human or technical sources. It is a time to be alone, to dream, to think, and to plan.

I love solitude. I can think of several situations when solitude was a memorable experience. I love traveling. We are so fortunate to be able to move around our world, for there is so much to see, hear, and smell. What a great experience it is to sit in a 747 with an organ and trumpet concerto coming through the headphones as clouds float below you; I feel as if I am lost in space. I remember camping with friends in the Rocky Mountains. After the chores were completed, each person did his own thing before crawling into his sleeping bag to rest after a hard day. I walked up a ridge of mountains high above our campsite. As I sat on a large rock, a strange feeling came over me, one I do not have the good fortune to experience often. I felt an incredible high with all the beautiful sights. I took a deep breath. The sun was slipping behind a distant range of mountains. To my left, a high peak was bathed in golden pink; a few clouds were outlined in brilliant red. The valleys before my eyes were bathed in purple shadows. I could barely hear the river which twisted and tumbled far below me. All around, the peaks stretched to infinity. It was calm, so incredibly calm. I felt so insignificant, so small, so perfectly alone. It was getting dark. I looked at my watch and more than two hours had slipped away. It seemed only a moment. I could barely move.

Paul Tillich thinks that solitude is glory in being alone,

while loneliness is pain in being alone. He feels that one way of overcoming loneliness is by experiencing solitude, by being able to spend some time alone. I truly agree with him. We should cherish the experience, even though many of us find it a challenge. We prefer routine and become creatures of habit. But during moments of peace and aloneness we begin to question and doubt. We begin to look at the meaning of life, as well as question the meaning of self. These are profound and challenging experiences. Is it not easier to chat on the phone, sip a drink, or to watch a movie? If we do not experience aloneness, then we probably do not experience something very precious in life, something that holds fear and doubt as well as happiness and certainty. Ideally, all of us should be able to find some time to spend in solitude. Even though we are born alone and die alone, we should be able to find other moments in our busy lives to be by ourselves. Twice is not enough.

seven

Coping with
Loneliness:
What We Usually Do

Most people have a hard time coping with loneliness. Often when certain events occur, they feel loneliness approaching like a mild form of depression. Some people are able to face the feeling of loneliness head on. They experience it as they would experience feelings of fear, frustration, or anger. Some people fear the onset of loneliness with a passion. Others accept it as fate in life, while others try to avoid it like a dreaded disease. I will now discuss some of the mechanisms that people use to defend themselves against loneliness and its accompanying emotions. I will also mention some of the positive values achieved when one confronts his loneliness.

What are defense mechanisms? They are physical or verbal actions taken to protect our somewhat fragile selves. Since part of what we are is determined by what people think and say about us, we tend to protect our real selves from others. Whatever we do, we want to be certain that our egos remain intact. The actions and explanations that we employ as defense mechanisms are socially acceptable. For example, instead of accepting the fact that the real reason we were unable to go to college was because of a lack of intelligence, we explain to others that we decided that school had very little to offer us. The more certain we are about ourselves, the less we will rely on defenses. The less we know and think of ourselves, the more defenses we will use to cope with reality.

Each of us unconsciously uses certain defense mechanisms that help to protect and preserve our self-image. Defense mechanisms are probably necessary for our survival. On the other hand, they can be quite debilitating if we are constantly making excuses, instead of taking risks and assuming responsibility. Since defense mechanisms operate mainly at the unconscious level, we may not be aware of our behavior or the reason for its occurrence.

The use of defense mechanisms is a normal human reaction, but when they are used to an extreme, they begin to interfere with the preservation of self-worth. Protecting the self from anxiety or a loss of self-esteem is the main purpose of defense mechanisms. However, the price paid for this protection is the distortion of reality. These mechanisms are like coats of armor. The more coats you have, the more protection you have from the outside world, but your perception is limited by the layers around you. On the other hand, how can you stand naked in the world? You usually resent having some person call your attention to some of the defense mechanisms you use, because more often than not, it implies something negative about your behavior.

Another problem arises with calling attention to what a person is doing to cope with reality. The individual who "tells" is often afraid of the other person's reaction. There is both fear of hurting someone and fear of being rejected because of that hurt. Not only is this true with regard to a defense mechanism one uses, but it is also true given the problem of loneliness. How can a person be told that he is lonely and his problem is not being dealt with in a rational way? This is particularly difficult since the lonely individual may be suffering from feelings of insecurity or inadequacy. I have struggled with this problem for many years. Can I be totally honest with a friend in discussing problems that I feel he is not coping with in a rational manner? How can I be certain that my perceptions of him are accurate? I may see problems because of my own hang-ups, so it may relate to me, not him. However, if I care for a friend, then I am being dishonest when I do not convey my feelings and perceptions, however accurate or inaccurate they may be.

I appreciate the perceptions of my close friends whose concern and caring means a great deal. I do not think we have to play the role of guru with people who are close to us. As human beings, we simply want someone we can trust and confide in, someone who will share our feelings and not be judgmental in the process. As a rule, I think women are better than men in this area.

Let us now examine some of the common defense mechanisms used to cope with loneliness as well as other related problems.

PRETENDING THE PROBLEM
DOES NOT EXIST

SUE: I hear that you are really lonely since your breakup with Jane.

SAL: Oh no, I am fine! Life is no different from what it was before. By the way, how is your brother doing in his work?

We have heard the expression that "love is blind," or that the ostrich buries his head in the sand. These expressions are exemplified in the mechanism of denying reality. Sometimes we manage to avoid unpleasant realities by refusing to acknowledge them or by simply avoiding them. How often we refuse to discuss unpleasant topics by ignoring them or by changing the subject. We do not like criticism. When something unpleasant is said, we change the subject. Basically, we sometimes refuse to face some of our real problems. One of these may be loneliness.

As I have mentioned before, I think many people are lonely. If I confronted them with this problem, the majority would probably deny it; this is somewhat akin to admitting to defeat or failure in life. We tend to look away with a smile to hide the hurt inside. We may see a person whose marriage is on shaky grounds while he pretends that all is well and rosy. A man who experiences constant failure at work expresses delight in his success. Sometimes a lonely person can be spotted in the crowd as the one who laughs and talks the loudest. Moreover, one situation does not lead to one specific form of behavior. I may hear somebody saying, "My mother is not a lonely person and she is the loudest person at any cocktail party. What you say is not true." Certainly this may be the case, because there are always individual differences and exceptions. However, when I observe people's behavior, I wonder why one person wants to be belle of the ball while another is quite content simply to have a ball.

Regardless of how one interprets behavior, denying loneliness prevents one from seeing things in their proper perspective. It does not enable that person to grow and reach higher plateaus of life leading to maturity. One takes a huge stride forward when he is able to admit his loneliness to himself and to others.

DAYDREAMING

SAL: (Lost in a daydream) And now ladies and gentlemen, I would like to present to you the very likeable, the very popular, Mr. Congeniality, Sal Sampson!

How many times have you imagined yourself next to Raquel Welch, or if you are female, next to Paul Newman, driving through the countryside in a Rolls Royce, then parking in a lovely field of flowers under the shade of a tree and then . . . darn it, the phone rings and your boss calls. Back to reality you go! Such is the world of fantasy or what people usually refer to as daydreaming.

We often regard the child who sits in the back row of a classroom staring out the window as a classic example of a daydreamer. He is the student the teacher cannot motivate, and the one who is building castles in the sky. Adults do their share of daydreaming as well. As in the case of other defense mechanisms, fantasy can be a constructive experience where the excitement motivates us to higher goals in real life. A productive fantasy can thus be a way of solving problems. Furthermore, the ability to remove ourselves from the reality of everyday life to a world of fantasy can be good therapy. Sometimes when I drive my Chevette, I dream of owning a Rolls Royce with a ski rack on it. When I retreat into this fantasy, a smile spreads across my face.

But what about the lonely person? Fantasy can be a very good experience if it does not get out of hand and become a nonproductive activity compensating for a lack of achievement. When you sit and dream about some of the steps you might take to lessen your loneliness, you are using the experience as a constructive tool. You may imagine yourself in a social situation where you can meet people, or think of having some people over to your house for an evening. You can imagine the person you would like to be and how you might strive to make this image become reality. Good things often begin as a dream.

On the other hand, you can dream of being Cinderella, going to the ball, finding a prince and living happily ever after in fantasy land. You can dream of the fun everybody is having at the discos and movies while poor little you stays home and watches dull television programs. Fantasy can really get out of hand when you are extremely frustrated, or have failed to improve your personal situation. At these times you should be somewhat wary of the solutions that come to mind. If your loneliness is intense, your daydreams probably do not represent reality too well.

You must not feel that you are abnormal if you indulge in daydreaming. No matter who you are, if you use this defense mechanism as a temporary escape, you are in pretty good shape. It is only when you revert to fantasy as a permanent excuse that you lose touch with reality and get closer to the life of Superman, Elizabeth Taylor, or the Six Million Dollar Man.

PROVING THAT YOU CAN DO IT

SUE: Come on over and meet my cousin Elsie, Sal.

SAL: I really don't have time tonight. I must finish my ninety-fifth novel today so that I can get my gold medal and certificate for "top reader of the century" from the library.

Compensating is attempting to hide the existence of an undesirable characteristic by emphasizing a positive aspect. There are many examples of how this mechanism works. A person with poorly developed muscles may sometimes compensate by increased effort to achieve motor skills. I know a man who had polio when he was a child. The disease did not leave him crippled, but affected the development of his leg muscles. This person is a tiger when he participates in sports. When he plays tennis, he is as agressive as a professional player. When cross-country skiing, he measures the success of his trip by the distance he can cover. Other examples include the boy who is not brilliant academically but is an extremely capable football player, or a girl who is unattractive but develops a terrific personality. Compensation allows us to put our best foot forward.

A lonely person may use compensation as an effective defense mechanism. Consider the lonely man who does not dance, converse well, or drink beer. You would not find him in many discothéques. He seeks activities which do not involve people. Music and sleeping might seem appropriate alternatives. A lonely person who feels unattractive and rejected might turn to sexual promiscuity for love and affection. He then feels needed and wanted. The overall result could lead to anger and guilt. Loneliness can settle into his life with great intensity and to avoid the unpleasant feeling he may indulge in more promiscuity. Sometimes there is very little chance to turn back.

Another example might be the lonely person who never has had a chance to form a relationship, so turns instead to books as a compensational device. Although reading is a very valuable pastime enjoyed by millions of people, it becomes a problem when we rely exclusively on the world of books for our comfort and aid. We can always be busy in the evening because we have fifteen novels started and there are many others that are waiting to be read. Unfortunately, books as exciting as they may be, will never replace true human interaction.

Many people who experience Loneliness I compensate by engaging in activity which lessens the frustrations of low self-esteem. Loneliness and frustration can lead to excessive eating, drinking, or both. Comfort is sought in oral gratification. Frustration can also lead to escape, violence, and hostility. Underneath the defense mechanisms, one finds a shrunken self. Loneliness I and insecurity form another unpleasant combination. People who lack self-confidence often brag about themselves. No matter where I go, I frequently hear people boasting about their achievements, but they hardly ever ask how I am doing. A safe rule to follow is never to tell people how great you are; let them find out for themselves.

We are constantly comparing ourselves to others in terms of

possessions, status, and forms of achievement. For many, this can be a positive incentive to be at least average, to try and improve, or to attain greater heights. We use compensation in moderation to achieve some of these goals. When it hinders our progress, or leads to antisocial forms of behavior, then we are using this defense mechanism in a negative way.

EXPLAINING YOUR LIFE AWAY

SUE: What really happened between you and Jane?

SAL: Well, what a pain! She couldn't stand the way I danced the hustle, and she complained that my left thumb was smaller than my right one, which affected my table manners.

Here we have an example of a very commonly used defense mechanism. Children are very quick to rationalize, but adults are also susceptible to this ploy. Rationalization is like making excuses. It persuades us to do something that we probably should not be doing. In addition, rationalization also makes disappointment easier to bear if we do not achieve our goals. Disappointment is minimized. When a person is rationalizing, he is providing some socially acceptable reasons for his behavior.

When a student stays in the cafeteria and plays cards instead of going to class, his excuse may be that the teacher and class are boring anyway, so why go. When that same person does poorly on the examination, he explains that he isn't surprised because he didn't study. If he were caught cheating, he would probably explain that everyone else is cheating, so why shouldn't he? His failures on exams are probably due to his lack of motivation or interest, but the real reason does not sound convincing as his more socially acceptable rationalization.

One can imagine how a lonely person might react to his emotional situation. By simple rationalization, he could invent reasons to explain his condition, and thus soften the blow. There are numerous excuses as to why he is not attempting to find any solution to his loneliness. An individual who is afraid of socializing or meeting people explains that he hates noise, smoke, dancing, and drinking. Furthermore, there is very little time to socialize because of a heavy work load, and homework to be done every night. If some friends suggest an introduction to a new girl in the office, he declines on the grounds that she is probably like all the girls he has met in the past, demanding and expensive. At the other extreme, a very lonely but hyperactive person might disregard your advice to slow down and be more reflective by claiming that silence is deadly and idleness is sinful.

Past experience plays an important role in present behavior. If I had been engaged two or three times to different girls and each girl ran away a day or two before the wedding, I would be somewhat careful about my next move. However, some people never learn from their mistakes. They repeat the same behavior to lessen some of their loneliness and to prove that their self-image has not been beaten into the ground. Moreover, an individual can be very lonely and depressed at such times and remain in the same spot out of fear of further rejection. Even if a person has not been severely jilted, he may create elaborate excuses as to why he does not want to get involved. He might explain that he is not very exciting or handsome, and that is why people never want to be his friend. On the other hand, he might also say that no one is good enough for him because he is in a class of his own and thus quite unapproachable.

Whatever the situation, it is difficult to know exactly when one is being fairly objective and when one is rationalizing. We can assume the individual is using his defense mechanism if he reacts angrily or defensively when his excuses are probed. If we know a person is always searching for reasons to justify his actions, then we can be quite certain that he is employing rationalization.

How can you tell if you use this defense mechanism frequently? You should reflect as honestly as you can and determine how much truth your rationalizations contain. Be honest with yourself. If excessive rationalization continues, then you are paying the price of self-deception. Some of the reasons you give for your actions may not make you a liar; often they seem very real. One can only imagine what the net result would be if rationalization were carried to an extreme.

GETTING AWAY FROM IT ALL

SAL: Hello, Sue. I have ten minutes. How about going for a drive, having a couple of beers, and just doing some talking. I hate sitting at home!

SUE: Are you sure you won't be bored?

When we think of escape, we often think of somebody running away from prison. In everyday life the person who escapes is avoiding or running away from some aspect of his life. By removing himself from the situation, he temporarily avoids the familiar stimuli which cause negative behavior. He may escape in thought but not in reality. Escape does not always involve mobility. It may be a simple form of avoidance in the mind.

Have you ever tried to phone someone who has experienced marital breakdown? He is often difficult to reach. By being on the go the person is keeping his mind off his problems, especially the problem of loneliness. He can be visiting people, going to discothéques or bars, and constantly looking for dates. I know one person who represents a classic case of escapism. His wife and children left the country, and he was left alone. At times he would take drugs to cope with his loneliness and despair. He was hardly ever at home. Sometimes he had two dates in one evening with girls that were not really worth the time and money in his estimation. Seeing a movie or sitting in a restaurant having coffee was more appealing than sitting at home and enjoying his own company.

Sleep is another wonderful form of escape for many people. Your loneliness does not plague your mind once you are asleep. True, you may toss and turn in the middle of the night, but for many people there is satisfaction in staying in bed as long as possible. I know a couple who used to sleep all day Saturday, then quickly rush off to the supermarket to shop before it closed. I cannot imagine anyone loving sleep that much! If you are prowling the night until four in the morning and sleeping past noon, you are escaping during the day. How exciting your life must be.

The whole world of drugs and alcohol is an escape from reality. Even a temporary high is better than no high at all for some people. The painful world is not quite so unbearable when you give your system artificial assistance. Cocaine and alcohol are current forms of escape. In fact, when I think of a lonely person who cannot escape physically, the bottle and the bottomless glass come to mind. Maybe this image comes from films I have seen, but unfortunately one does not have to go to the movies to witness this phenomenon. Again, I cannot generalize that all people who drink are lonely, and certainly not all lonely people drink. But there is always the danger that when pressures mount up, one may reach for the bottle.

In modern society, drinking is so much a part of our lives. A social drink may only be a start. Before we know it, we can be leading lives similar to those of millions around the world. People who recognize the problem in friends and acquaintances are afraid because excessive drinking can touch all social classes, either sex, any age, and today affects many teenagers as well. I need not emphasize the dangers of alcohol, because a good number of us have had or have seen people with this problem. Despite the after-effects, the immediate escape is a great relief to most drinkers.

Needless to say, not all lonely people seek escape and those that do may not necessarily be lonely. Escape can be a welcome temporary panacea for tension, fear, and boredom. One often hears, especially from older people that one of the best ways to lessen the strain of loneliness is to keep very busy. How can you feel that numbness of loneliness for any period of time when you are always on the go and always busy doing something? Sometimes I wonder about our society. Maybe we are driven to seek financial success because we tend to remain idle for very, very short periods of time. How guilty people feel when they remain inactive for several hours. They immediately think of the dozens of things they must do. There are tires to repair, bicycles to fix, dishes to wash, and so on. We are ridden with guilt if we are not always active. We must at least give the appearance of being busy.

I often look at the neighbors puttering in their gardens. Instead of carrying one shovelful of dirt, they use a little scoop so they can make five trips instead of one. Instead of getting down on their knees and weeding the entire garden in a couple of hours, they wander from patch to patch pulling an occasional weed. Instead of taking the clothes from the line or dryer, folding them, and putting them away, many women move them at least three times from one place to another. We are slaves to activity!

Is there anything good or bad, right or wrong, with escape? Some say this it occupies their time, takes their mind off their worries, and eases pain. Escape enables them to function, and often it is not a matter of choice. They are hardly conscious of why they are behaving the way they do. Only with awareness can behavior be modified.

MASKING WHAT I REALLY FEEL

SUE: I can't stand the way Jane dresses. Her skirts are too short, her makeup too thick, and she acts like a tease. She's disgusting!

SAL: Ah, jealousy, the green-eyed monster!

Examples of this defense mechanism can sometimes lead to a laugh or a chuckle, but not from the person who is laughed at. A person will often develop behavioral patterns and attitudes which are the exact opposite of how he feels. By means of this mechanism the individual can suppress desires and impulses which, under ordinary conditions, could get him into trouble, especially if he carried them out.

The quotation "The lady doth protest too much, methinks" falls into the category of overreaction. Whenever I hear a person expounding an idea until it is almost beaten to death, I wonder why he feels so strongly about it. Is it not a case of overreacting? A couple of years ago, many people in one province chuckled when a person in charge of movie censorship was charged with a sexual offense because he was fooling around with teenage girls. Sometimes we listen to some crusader who is out to save souls. He preaches about the horrors of rock records, the sinful pastime of watching movies, and the evils of dancing, necking, or heaven forbid, making love. One almost immediately thinks of overreaction. Deep down inside this person may have the desires he is condemning.

Another example is a teacher I knew who was going steady and became pregnant. When she had the child, she practically smothered the boy with overprotection. A baby sitter was never allowed to look after him, he never went outside because the temperature was either too hot or too cold, and she hardly let the child out of her sight. Subconsciously she probably felt deep guilt, since she had not really wanted the child. Beware of someone who would like to "hug you to death." Just ask for a peck on the cheek. Let the boa constrictors stay in the jungle where they belong.

What about the lonely person? In order to hide his feelings of loneliness he may develop a "who cares how everybody else feels?" attitude. He shows little concern for others and keeps his emotions under control. Deep down he is craving for acceptance and the "oh, who cares?" has more significance to it than meets the eye. He is laughing on the outside and crying on the inside. His actions depict a fun-loving person but they hide a soul that is crying for help.

The main drawback to the defense mechanism of overreaction is that it can be self-deceptive. It can lead to rigid and exaggerated beliefs and fears that could be a big stumbling block when dealing with one's own values as well as the values of others. If I were to compare it with the other defense mechanisms, I would say overreaction is one of the most serious and problematic.

BLAMING THE OTHER PERSON

SAL: Sue, bring me that file and don't walk as if your legs were tied together. Melissa, I can't bear your sagging pantyhose. Can't you buy the right size? Shape up or ship out!

SUE: (to Melissa) I wonder what his mother fed him this morning?

Displacement refers to a shift of emotion from one person or object to a more neutral person. For example, a man is angry with his boss; he cannot swear or show any outward emotion because he fears losing his job. When he gets home, he lets off steam by yelling at his wife or children. He realizes that his children will not strike back; they can only mumble "grouch" under their breaths. The pent-up emotion is usually triggered by a very small incident. Normally, when the child drops a toy there would be no response from the father. However, given the stressful work situation, the noise from the dropped toy will trigger a torrent of abuse and anger in the father. A child who has been severely reprimanded by his mother may direct his hostility toward his teacher. The recipient of the somewhat unexpected behavior may be alarmed and dismayed by the verbal bombardment.

How may a lonely person exhibit displacement? Take, for example, a person who is angry at a friend because he truly holds him responsible for the situation. Tom may blame his mother because there were numerous times when she did not approve of his dating and insisted on having a full account of all his activities. When Tom was ready to go on vacation, his mother became terribly ill, and needed someone to look after her. Now Tom is thirty-five years old and living with his seventy-five-year-old mother. He feels useless as a person. His anger toward his mother is displaced toward his job partner and to the children on the street who sometimes cross his lawn. The children run, curse him, and call him an old ogre.

Displacement can be a valuable defense mechanism because one is able to vent emotions without risking the loss of love, as in the case of the mother, or retaliation, as in the case of the boss. Sometimes, the individual is not even aware of the person for whom the feelings were originally intended. For example, when Tom lashes out at his colleagues, he may not be aware that his anger is intended for his mother. Whatever the situation, the process enables him to release emotions which otherwise would be bottled up inside and possibly lead to other physical and mental symptoms. Showing your emotions is better than keeping them bottled up inside. However, showing your emotions by displacement may not always be the best solution to your problem.

If an individual uses displacement continuously, he may avoid many situations that should be handled differently. For example, if Tom feels anger toward his mother, it probably would be wise for him to express and discuss his feelings with her, since his mother is the person who elicited the feelings in the first place. After all, why displace his emotions toward others who do not know what is happening at home.

AVOIDING RISK

SAL: Since Judy left me, I simply refuse to get involved in another love affair.

SUE: But Sal, not all girls are like Judy. I would like you to meet my cousin Gladys.

An individual uses this defense mechanism in an attempt to reduce fears and needs by withdrawing into a world of passivity. Because of the disappointments and hurts that he experienced in the past, he lowers his level of aspiration and his level of emotional involvement as well. Take, for example, the man who has had a bad love affair and as a result is very cautious about getting involved in another close relationship. He may even use other defense mechanisms, such as rationalization when he explains that he is getting too old to be involved.

In this world we find people who appear to be quite self-sufficient but are usually victims of anxiety and loneliness. Because the world is not a place for easy sailing, they frequently receive many bruises and knocks that lead to emotional scars. As a result, they are usually unable to receive or give affection. This type of situation may result when divorced people contemplate remarriage. It is almost impossible to survive marital breakup without emotional scars. Although some people escape the hurt by racing into a new relationship before the dust settles around them, the majority are cautious with new involvements. In fact, some are afraid to trust and to risk. After all, if failure has occurred once, what proof is there that it will not happen again? Because we are fragile creatures, we must protect ourselves. One way is to continue to exist at the expense of emotional insulation.

In the world of loving, to be emotionally involved means that one must be willing to take risks. After all, the possibility exists that when we give our affection to an individual, it may be rejected. Sometimes we must prepare ourselves for more tragic situations such as accidents or death. What can we do? We can be truly traumatized by these experiences. If we continue to live under a dark umbrella, we seldom see the sun. Like flowers, we need the sun to bloom. So we take risks, and the rewards of emotional involvement are often well worth the risks, even though we know that there may be disappointments in life and with the disappointments, pain and sorrow.

There is the danger that we have already become rocks or islands. The more we isolate ourselves, the more we become islands unto ourselves. When we give up hope, we cease to grow and only death reaps the rewards. Life is too short for us to withdraw, to be tossed around and buffeted by loneliness. To grow and survive as human beings, it is necessary to relate to ourselves and to other people emotionally. This involves risk and is well worth it.

THE LIMITATIONS
OF DEFENSE MECHANISMS

There are several ideas we should keep in mind when we examine defense mechanisms in ourselves or in others. One should not think of defense mechanisms as being abnormal, whatever normal may mean. We use one or more defense mechanisms in certain situations; there is no clear-cut choice as to which defense will be used. In general, defense mechanisms are quite desirable because they protect and guard us. They reduce many of our conflicts and many of our worries from hour to hour, day to day, week to week. But if some of our conflicts are not resolved, our ability to function could be more seriously impaired.

On the other hand, we must remember that many of our defense mechanisms are learned. We are not born with them. Once learned, they operate almost automatically. A given stimulus can very quickly put our defenses into operation. For example, if your friend comments about your sitting around and doing nothing worthwhile, you may quickly reply that you are not feeling well and your headache is not allowing you to see straight. If in fact this reply is an excuse, you are falling back on a defense mechanism.

Another important factor is the number of defenses we have and the frequency of their use. If you frequently operate under a multitude of defenses, you should realize that your protection is paid for by a distortion of reality. Like a clam, you open up once in a while to see what the real world is like. The problem with this is that you never really grow as a person. You keep hiding from reality from day to day. You cannot leave one level of life and move to a higher one. You tend to stay on one plateau and can only look up at people on a higher level. It is never too late. Although the climb may result in a few falls, a few bruises and a few tears, it is still within reach for most of us. All we have to do is try.

Such is the case of loneliness. On the negative side, we can forever give excuses and reasons for our lonely feeling. It may be a temporary or a permanent state with some of us. However, there can be some good associated with temporary loneliness. Positive results are achieved when we do not depend on our defense mechanisms to survive, but instead face the challenge of our lonely state.

ABANDONING DEFENSES
AND DISCOVERING
THE VALUE OF LONELINESS

If you do not hide behind your shell, you can find that experiencing some loneliness can be a positive experience. Loneliness is a condition of existence which can lead to deeper awareness, sensitivity, and insights into one's own life. There can be some soul-searching if you do not run away from life. During these moments there is a sense of separateness where you stand apart from the world and see yourself as a unique person. Self-confrontations can give you the strength to exist on a truly human plane. Your identity comes into perspective. After all, how can you think and create if you are not alone?

It has been said that if you do not experience loneliness you do not know what sensitivity is. Loneliness is experiencing the senses, because you are able to hear, feel, and touch with greater clarity. To be receptive to life is in a sense to be lonely, for at such a time your senses are heightened. It is during times of loneliness that you are truly aware, you discover life, discover who you are, what you really want, what existence means to you, and what your relationship is to others. You can see for the first time truths that in the past have been obscured. Many distortions become more transparent.

Facing loneliness without defenses can open avenues to an expanding life. You can discover new meanings, new values that have not been allowed to enter your reality. New approaches to life can be accepted with renewed hope and vitality. Loneliness may allow you to put more effort into your desires, your hopes, and your problems. The net result can be a richer and fuller life.

If you live by the idea that you should never be lonely, then you alienate yourself from your own capacity to be lonely and from any possibility of social relationships and empathy. It is not the loneliness per se that separates you from others, but the terror of the loneliness and your constant effort to escape this feeling. You must learn to experience and to suffer some loneliness. However, it just does not happen. You must devote energy to such an endeavor.

For all of us, loneliness is as much a part of reality as life and death. The more we try to avoid and fear loneliness, the more we fear life itself. To say we are never lonely is to say that we never live. We *are* lonely people. If we can experience loneliness, we can grow as people with new promise, maturity, hope, and love.

However, I do not want to convince people that loneliness is a great experience or one that shouldn't be missed. What I am trying to say is that since some loneliness is inevitable, we can use some of these hours of solitude and aloneness to enable us to progress in our lives. It is necessary to reexamine our strengths and abilities in order to lessen the burden of Loneliness I. Very little seems to happen without effort; we do have a choice either to accept who we are and do nothing or accept who we are and attempt to become better people. The same is true with Loneliness II. We can accept our present situation, accept our lack of meaningful relationships, and continue to be partners with the silent company, or we can use our loneliness as a time for thought and contemplation. We can deal with our present and try to perceive some clarity and direction in our lives. Let us now examine some of the strategies we can employ to alleviate at least some of the harshness of Loneliness I as well as the sting of Loneliness II.

eight
Overcoming
Loneliness I:
Helping Oneself

One can easily criticize an individual's shortcomings but offer very little in the line of alternatives. I believe there never is only one solution to problems found in our lives. However, the method we use to jump over hurdles and the answers we get do affect us for years to come. We harvest what we sow. The rewards come only when we do some thinking and planning, then follow through with action.

Loneliness has many facets and may be handled in many different ways. Whereas one person will accept his situation and do nothing about it, another will totally deny that he is even lonely. Another person handles loneliness by escaping, rationalizing, or using any number of defense mechanisms that he has learned. Finally, one can admit that he is lonely, feel all its impact, and during this emotionally trying experience learn about himself and what to do to lessen the burden. Who is to say that any one person is doing the right or wrong thing? After all, what is good for me may not be very satisfactory for you. What works for me may not work for you. We are as different in our emotional components as we are in outward appearances. There is no single recipe for happiness and there is no easy road to a beautiful life. We can only achieve what we really want by striving toward that goal. For some it is a small task but for others it is a slow and painful experience. The answer lies in our desire to want to do something with our lives.

Thus, regardless of the multitude of variables that affect everyday life, I think there are suggestions that can be offered which apply to a large number of people. This does not mean that every person will necessarily benefit or agree with suggestions that are offered. Some people benefit from advice given to them, some avoid it on principle, and still others ignore any verbal assistance. There are even some who could really care less. I find that people do not always accept suggestions at face value. For some reason they always have some suspicion that they are being led down the garden path.

If we at least try to listen to ourselves as well as to others, we may grow as individuals. There is very little reward to be gained by sitting around and complaining about our situation. I believe that we have freedom to make decisions, and there are people who take advantage of this situation in a positive way. Others abuse their freedom and remain stationary or regress to earlier forms of behavior. Others do not even know any freedom exists and simply tolerate their situation.

If only a few of us paused for a few minutes once in a while and realized how quickly time passes, how the hours and days and years fly by. How short life really is! We must live every hour as if it were our last, knowing it is gone forever. Realizing this, some of us might attempt to do something with ourselves. For instance, many people struggle, save, and merely survive for years, so they can enjoy their old age. However, it is necessary to make the best of what we have at every stage in life. Since we are unable to turn to the past or future, the important time is now.

I adhere to the basic premise that loneliness can only be overcome by dealing with the self. The first step is to accept yourself as you are now; every day starts with liking yourself. You must honestly enjoy your own company and regard yourself as a unique individual. This does not solve all your problems, but it is a good beginning. Some people regard this basic step as an ego trip or selfish behavior that only a child can indulge in. I do not agree. I do not mean that you should stand in front of a mirror and blow kisses at yourself, or worry only about yourself. I mean you must really care about yourself as a person, someone who deserves to be alive.

If you like yourself, then you start off on a firm foundation. You have a base from which you can grow and develop. There is hope. Remember, liking myself does not mean that I am "selfish" and no one else matters. This is neurotic behavior that should be avoided. Of course, I cannot live without other people, and I need good friends. I need other people to give me reinforcement. In order to grow, I need the helping hands of others who are important to me.

Furthermore, we do not have to be extraordinary in order to like ourselves. If we feel we are nothing, then it becomes quite difficult to feel good about ourselves. We should work on our positive qualities and not on our faults. Feeling good about oneself does not just happen. If I tell myself that I am great, yet no other person feels this is so, I may be standing under an umbrella with only a few spokes to protect me. I can dissolve no matter how wonderul I think I am.

If you can accept yourself and truly like yourself, then it becomes easier to move to the next step and reach out to others. You possess some of the basic security needed to move ahead. On the other hand, if you like only yourself and do not establish any meaningful relationships, you stand a chance of missing something very beautiful, something that money cannot buy. Friendship, with its warmth, caring, and love is very special, very human.

Remember, it is important not to deceive yourself, since narcissism can be a false type of security. I know people who think they are the greatest; they act and talk "big," and think the world revolves around them. Such people are quite annoying, and they don't have a prayer in heaven of reaching out in their present state. These people are really very insecure, and they seem to be crying out for help. It is very important to be honest with yourself; don't pretend you are a tiger if you are a pussy cat.

Let us not forget the concepts of loneliness presented earlier. First, we have Loneliness I which refers to the lonely self. This is the loneliness all of us wish to avoid. Chronic loneliness takes its toll of human emotions and interactions. In order to conquer some of this loneliness, it is necessary to examine our self-concepts, to examine who we are, and to work toward self-improvement and the self-confidence so many of us lack. It is very difficult to be objective with oneself; in fact, we often tend to avoid any soul-searching. But if we reach a point in our lives when we feel good about ourselves, and we honestly possess self-confidence, we are then ready to move out and risk relationships. We need some relationships in order to survive without the company of Loneliness II. It is difficult to deal with one's self and to strive toward improvement, but it is no easy task to reach out to people and to establish meaningful relationships. The depth of the relationship will depend on the level of growth we have achieved when we form a specific relationship.

Thus I believe there is something you can do to alleviate your lonely existence. You begin by conquering Loneliness I which can then lead to an attack on Loneliness II. The more Loneliness I you are able to overcome, the less severe you will find Loneliness II. Shades of one affect the other. We can use our lonely state as a time to ponder, pause, and contemplate. Obviously, we do not require loneliness to think and act. We can certainly use our brain in other situations, free from emotional interference. Whatever arguments we use, we can and do function in the presence of the lonely company; however, we can do better without it.

On different occasions people have asked me what they can do to lessen their loneliness. I have no easy solutions, and think that telling people what to do is not the answer. I can only offer an approach to be considered and have taken the liberty to give suggestions as well as exercises that may help overcome both Loneliness I and II. I further suggest the book *How to Succeed at Love* by M. Zwell, whose exercises I found both interesting and useful; they also serve as a model for the exercises that I provide in this chapter and Chapter 9.

OVERCOMING LONELINESS I

When we are describing a person's self-image, we usually refer to what the person is, what others think of him, what he thinks of himself, and how he regards others' opinions of him. Basically, self-image is formed by both "you" and "others." You need feedback from other individuals to help you form a picture of yourself.

Self-concept and Loneliness I are closely related. The better your self-image, the less Loneliness I you experience. In fact, if you feel good about yourself and your total picture is impressive, you are on the road to various achievements. Like powerful fuel, a positive self-concept propels you forward with confidence.

I honestly feel that one's positive self-concept is the greatest asset that an individual can possess. Like good health, it can see one through some very stormy days. Even when the clouds are heavy, it is still possible to see some rays of light. All wealth, beauty, fame, and talent fall to the wayside when our self-image begins to crumble.

We human beings ask ourselves questions that are related to our self-esteem. We often wonder what a person thinks of us when we say or do something. We might even take a minute out of our busy lives and ask ourselves how we are doing, or merely look at ourselves in the mirror and ask ourselves such questions as: Who really am I? Am I any good? Am I okay? Am I normal?

It is of interest to note that we really do not know who we are without the help of others. Part of our definition of self-concept relies on the feedback we get from other people. No matter how great we are or how great we think we are, if the feedback we get from other people is to the contrary, we have no choice but to call them liars, ignore them, or listen and think about what they have said.

In order to know who we are, we must learn to be honest with ourselves, and we must learn to listen. Although this is easy to say or write, it is extremely difficult to do in everyday life. We never get the total picture of self if we ignore our own honest evaluation or if we ignore the evaluation of others. The evaluation that comes from others is important if it comes from people who are important to us, such as parents, teachers, peers, friends, and family members. Certainly we feel our adrenalin flowing when a stranger yells at our driving; however, the feeling is not the deep, lasting impression we experience when it comes from someone close to us.

As human beings, we are constantly comparing ourselves to

others. We have certain ideas about our worth. We feel superior to some people, but at the same time inferior to others. Most often we compare ourselves with people whose abilities and talents are similar to ours. It is difficult to enhance our self-concept when we feel inferior to our peers. Often we excel in one or two areas so we can emphasize our strong points and underplay some of our weaker points. We want to enhance our self-image whenever possible.

As human beings, we protect ourselves very wisely. Most of us set certain goals or aspirations during our lifetime. We are wise if we set our levels of aspiration fairly realistically. For example, I might feel I can achieve B's in two courses. If in fact I receive two A's, I exceed my level of expectation and enhance my self-concept. Not only am I good, but I am in fact very good. However, this is only one aspect of my life. As a human being, I have my successes and failures, my positive and negative points. If my successes outnumber my failures, then I do not fall short of my level of functioning in terms of my self-worth. If, on the other hand, my successes are shaky, the failure to achieve my goals may do little to enhance my total self-esteem. The balloon loses some air and slowly begins to descend. Unfortunately, in life going down is easier and faster than rising to greater heights. The self-image demands a certain amount of energy just to stay at one level.

Another premise I accept is the important role that parents and teachers play in the development of healthy self-concepts in children. When I look at my past, I cannot help but think how fortunate I was to have had parents who had extremely positive attitudes toward my self-worth, and a dozen teachers who had to be some of the greatest people who ever walked the face of this earth. My memories of school fill me with warmth. Not once do I remember a teacher ridiculing me, or pointing out my worthlessness. In fact they instilled in me a feeling of confidence that I feel is so necessary in life. Because of my positive experiences, I never was a lonely child. I would relive my childhood days without a second thought. I must thank the people who were responsible for my physical and emotional well-being. With this in mind, I hope that there are thousands of parents and teachers who are doing their share to help beautiful children from experiencing the sting of loneliness. If we can help

them in this stage of life, then we are helping them to cope with
some of the serious demands that they are bound to encounter in a
lifetime. There is so much to do and there is often so little time.

Exercises 1, 2 and 3 are presented to help individuals focus on
themselves. They can better know who they are and how they see
themselves as well as how they think others see them. The total
picture of self relates to self-concept.

Exercise 1:
Getting to Know Yourself

AIM: To improve your self-knowledge.

PROCESS: Complete the following sentences:

> Most days I feel . . .
> I am happy when . . .
> I am unhappy when . . .
> I enjoy . . .
> I dislike it when others . . .
> At present I feel . . .
> Tomorrow I would like to . . .
> I would like to . . .
> I feel good when . . .
> I am angry when . . .
> I feel sad when . . .
> I like people who are . . .
> I wish . . .
> If I could I would . . .
> What I want most in life is . . .
> If I could live my life again I would . . .
> My parents think (thought) I . . .
> If I could spend a lot of money I would . . .
> I have fun when . . .
> At work I am . . .
> If I could change my life I would . . .
> When I look at my life I feel . . .
> When I look at the future I feel . . .
> What I want in life is . . .
> I especially feel good about myself when . . .

RESULTS: What insights have you gained about yourself? Is there any
overall adjective that describes you as a person?

Exercise 2:
How You See Yourself

AIM: To discover how you view yourself.

PROCESS: Answer the following questions.

Are you pleased with your appearance?
What would you like to see different?
What would you like to accomplish?
What would you like to do better?
If you had more time, what would you do?
Is there anything more you would like to get out of life?
Do you have some secret ambition?
What has made you angry recently?
What makes you tense?
Are you frequently anxious?
What do you complain about?
With whom would you like to get along better?
What seems to block your advance in life?
What wears you out?
What are you wasting in life?
What is your attitude toward friends? Others?
How do you feel others react to you?
What complicates your life?
What change would you like to see in yourself?

RESULTS: The answers provided give you some idea of who you think you are. When you can be totally honest, then "who" you think you are, and the "who you are" are the same. We should strive for this in life.

Exercise 3:
How Others See You

AIM: To be aware of how others see us.

PROCESS: We often want to receive feedback from others who provide a better understanding of who we are. If what we are and what others see we are are similar, our self-knowledge has improved. Rate yourself and how you think a close friend would rate you in terms of the following characteristics: (1—high; 2—medium, 3—low)

You				Others		
1	2	3	Appearance	1	2	3
1	2	3	Intelligence	1	2	3
1	2	3	Friendliness	1	2	3
1	2	3	Humor	1	2	3
1	2	3	Empathy	1	2	3
1	2	3	Conscientiousness	1	2	3
1	2	3	Initiative	1	2	3
1	2	3	Honesty	1	2	3
1	2	3	Personality	1	2	3
1	2	3	Trustworthiness	1	2	3
1	2	3	Efficiency	1	2	3
1	2	3	Dependability	1	2	3
1	2	3	Thoughtfulness	1	2	3
1	2	3	Compassion	1	2	3

RESULTS: Often who we think we are is not the same as what others feel about us. Are the perceptions that others have of you similar to your own perceptions? Who do you think is more accurate? Why? Do you always accept what others say about you? How do you judge? Note that the more agreement, the clearer the picture we have of who we really are.

SELF-IMAGE AND PARENTHOOD

Although children do not experience all the traumas of everyday, adult worries, growing up is no easy task. Some very basic attitudes, values, and beliefs are formed during childhood. Children ask many questions, some of which refer to their own worth, their abilities, intelligence, and fears. As parents, we must give each child as much of ourselves as we can in order to foster the development of a positive self-concept. This is no easy task. For some it is a natural process, but for others the challenge is totally beyond their capabilities. How can a father praise his child if he was emotionally starved by his own parents when he was a child? How can one give when there is nothing to give? Parents who have a good self-concept can help their children. Parents who lack any sense of self-worth cannot, as a rule, give what is not present in themselves.

Children have one strike against them before they are born, in that they have no choice in choosing their parents. If a child happens to have parents who appreciate his presence and give him plenty of support, he can at least move from childhood to adulthood with some confidence. More than anyone else parents should exert a positive influence on their children. A child is at the mercy of adults; if he finds a situation unbearable, he fights, withdraws, or runs away.

There is very little a parent can do if he does not love his child. He can provide the child with many material objects, say sweet things to the child, and even pretend he loves him. However, all children seem to have a sixth sense and intuit meaning from words and actions. They know when attempts to reach them lack true affection. In addition to saying "I love you," prove it with a kiss and a hug.

More than anything, you must care for the child as you care for life itself. When a child falls, give him some sympathy. If a child is upset because of his friend, empathize with him. If he is afraid of mathematics, do not ignore the child's feelings. If he is excited and happy, be happy with him and don't tell him to be quiet. Remember that you are a child at heart; age does not make you old. One beautiful feature children have is their spontaneity. You can be completely natural with them and be totally accepted. Discipline is caring. Set limits for children because they need and want them.

Praise the child when praise is due. We as humans always speak out when something is wrong, when we disagree, or when we are angry. When all is going well we keep quiet. Probably the idea that "no news is good news" is carried too far. The praise must be honest, since false praise is worse than no praise at all. A job well done deserves credit. Do not nag, because children learn to ignore or to respond only to the nagging. Be firm and consistent with the child.

Children imitate their parents. How can you expect a child to do a lot of reading if you are in front of the television for twenty hours a day? If you want your child to read, it may be a good idea for you to pick up a book once in a while. If you preach the evils of drinking, don't hide the bottle and sneak a drink when the children are not looking. The same is true for smoking. Be honest about your addiction to tobacco. Tell them that you realize it is a bad habit and it may be dangerous to your health.

Be perceptive. I cannot for a moment understand why parents keep their children up until ten and eleven each night. Even adults often feel like going to bed at ten. Habits form quickly and they are very difficult to break. Parents wear themselves out by nagging their children about going to bed. Furthermore, the parents have little time for themselves. Often hostility sets in. I am appalled when I see parents keeping their little ones up when they should have been in bed for hours. When I see this happening, I feel some people would be better off with just pets.

Do not ridicule or put a child down. As difficult as it is to praise, it is so easy to scold a child for all his weaknesses. Naturally, the child cannot fight back. He accepts the abuse, takes it out on himself and others, or ignores the statement. This cuts away at his self-image until there is nothing left.

In general, a child's self-image is very important because life is difficult for him too. If he feels confident and good about himself, he can cope with the constant teasing he experiences from other children. Have you ever noticed how cruel children are to each other? If a child's self-image is fragile, he turns to his parents for strength. If the parents have little to offer, he merely copes with his life. Children are important. Give them all you have.

Exercise 4 focuses on children and their self-concepts. A number of ideas are presented which adults can use with their own children. It is to be hoped that your child will have all the positive experiences necessary for growth.

Exercise 4:
Self-Concept and Children

AIM: To enhance the self-concept of children.

PROCESS: The following statements add to the growth of positive self-image in children. The greater the number of "yes" responses, the better your contributions:

I frequently hug my child.
I try to use few "don't" statements.
I am firm with my children.
I practice what I preach.
I praise my child when praise is due.
I reprimand a child's actions rather than the child himself.

I acknowledge some of the changes I see in a child.
I tell a child what he can be, not what he can't be.
I practice empathy.
I listen to what the child is saying.
I play with my child.
I tell my child I love him.
I enjoy giving my child a kiss.
I am concerned where my child is.
I set limits.
I treat each as an individual.
I do not expect a child to be an adult.
I think children should be allowed to think like children.
I avoid nagging and complaining.
I am consistent.
I allow a child to show his emotions.

RESULTS: When you can provide positive feedback, as well as praise and empathy, you are enabling a child to grow. Do you find that certain acts are more difficult than others? Why? How does a child respond? Is it possible to change our behavior toward a child?

SELF-CONCEPT AND TEACHERS

After parents, I feel that teachers play the next most important role in the development of healthy self-concepts in children. Because children spend many hours and days with a classroom teacher, I consider the work they do of great importance, second only to that of a parent. Working with students at my university, I see dozens of young people who have the potential to become fantastic teachers.

However, there are teachers who contribute very little to the welfare of a student. In fact they probably dislike children. They regard teaching as just another job with good hours and long holidays. We still find teachers who ridicule students, have them stand in a corner, or make them stay after class when they misbehave. I have walked past classrooms where a student was sleeping in the back row. Sometimes teachers talk about all the little "brats" they have to cope with. Having taught for many years, I realize that not all students are pure gold. Sometimes they frazzle your nerves, but I have another version of the "hallway theory"; if a teacher does not contribute to the overall learning in a classroom, he should stand out in the hallway. It is extremely enlightening to meet a truly dedicated teacher, a human being, who takes pride in and enjoys every hour of his challenging work. We have hundreds of good teachers but unfortunately not enough of them in all of our schools.

Some students are extremely difficult to teach, let alone enjoy. They have been scarred by rejection and are often beyond reach. Such students are difficult to cope with, and all the teacher can do is attempt to relate to the child. There is no magic. If the child has been devastated emotionally, there is no simple cure. My suggestion is that one should attempt to reach the individual. If the student responds, it is worth the effort.

In order to assist the student, a teacher's work should affect both cognitive and affective learning. Certainly a child should learn as much material as he is capable of mastering. Knowledge helps to build one's idea of self-worth. For many children, academic achievement is closely related to their self-image. In addition, the teacher should be able to care as much as possible. Students need empathy and respect for their feelings. Sometimes it is very difficult to see the worth in a student who appears to have very little going for him. This is the person who needs the most attention and approval; however, he often gets only negative feedback. His self-concept suffers. The ground under his feet begins to shake. How can he like himself?

My advice to teachers who have little experience in the classroom is to be firm, friendly, and fair. I believe that if most teachers were aware of these characteristics and truly showed them in a natural manner, then students would be less likely to drop out.

I do not believe that permissiveness is to be desired at home, and neither do I think it is proper in the classroom. Discipline is one important part of teaching. If the teacher does not have the firmness required to handle students, behavioral problems may arise, and the class becomes chaotic. I remember teaching in a high school which had students from all walks of life. I couldn't believe that one teacher was driven up the wall every year by students who I thought were really not bad at all. By disciplining you gain respect, and your words hold more meaning for the student. Just as at home, students should know how far they can go. They will test you all the way. I remember a teacher in a rural school next to the one I attended. She was no more than five feet tall and ever so slight. She would look up at the six-footers and put them in their place time after time. She was incredible. You don't have to be a lion to get results.

Students like teachers who are friendly. They do not expect you to visit or to be their friend; they simply want someone they can converse with. A "hi" or a smile goes a long way with many children. If it is insincere it doesn't go over at all; if it is natural, then the effects are far-reaching. A student naturally feels elevated. It is like saying, "Hey, he noticed me and smiled. Isn't that great. I'm really somebody. He must think I'm okay." Up goes the self-concept. This student can then trust the teacher by talking, sometimes about a movie, but sometimes about problems that are affecting his life.

A teacher must be fair. This does not mean setting up a list of rules. It simply means he must treat students with equality and show as little favoritism as possible. The student wants to know where he stands. Why should he be able to chew gum today and yet tomorrow be told to scrape all the gum off the desks because he was caught chewing? One must avoid making teacher's pets and scapegoats. The students should know what your expectations are. Why take off five marks for each spelling mistake when you did not mention this prior to the test?

There are other teaching qualities that should be mentioned, such as a sense of humour, intelligence, and a generally pleasant personality. I might add, that in addition to the characteristics mentioned, a teacher must be natural and honest, a human being who can control all his fluctuations in moods and emotions. If, for example, Mr. Black had a few cross words with his wife prior to leaving for school, there is no need to use defense mechanisms and to take it out on the children. Mr. Black could explain that he is not in the best of humor, and the students should ignore his cutting remarks. Students begin to develop more trust, and the overall effects make for a healthier learning climate.

In order to facilitate learning, it is necessary to be authentic. You teach by contact; you must have your presence felt in the classroom. Putting the material across to the students is only part of your work. You must be genuine; the real you must be in the classroom. This means that if you are happy, you show your happiness, but if you are angry or frustrated, you show these feelings as well. Not only do you have to be in tune with yourself, but you must be tuned to the needs of the children as well. So many teachers appear to be insensitive to the wishes of their pupils. In addition, you must practice empathy. Place yourself in the other person's shoes once in a while. Talk as quietly to the children as you would to the school superintendent. As in all relationships, it is necessary to risk. If you are more open to the class, then students in turn will be more open with you. In this case, both the teacher and the class grow in the direction of positive self-worth. Everyone needs it for survival!

Many of the teachers I had were great people. Some had very little formal training, and some were not exactly Einsteins, but they cared for all of us. I remember some of the very positive remarks they said to me, some of the smiles, and the rewards I received for my academic achievements. They instilled in me a very positive attitude for learning and teaching. I recall how I felt when my sixth grade teacher said that I would probably be Prime Minister of Canada someday. I felt ten feet tall! I felt like a king! How different I would have felt had she remarked that I was worth peanuts and was wasting my time breathing.

Thus, I beg teachers to try. The feedback may not be immediate, but you can instill in your students the greatest gift of all, a liking for oneself and a feeling of being needed and worthwhile. As these people step out into life, some will succeed but some will fall by the way. At least having a sense of worth can pull them through lonely times when friends are few and nobody really seems to care. These are the times when loneliness pulls at the heart and the mind spins.

Exercise 5 allows the teacher to look at his actions and what effect they have on his students. The statements are related to the relationships teachers have with their students rather than the ability to teach academic subjects.

Exercise 5:
Teachers and Student Self-concept

AIM: To enhance the self-concept of students in a classroom setting.

PROCESS: As a humanistic teacher, rate yourself on a scale from 1 (high) to 3 (low) with regards to some of the statements about enhancing a student's self-concept.

I believe that administration usually stands in my way to be an effective teacher.

Other teachers give me support in my work.

I can be a good teacher in spite of obstacles in a school setting.

To be an effective teacher, one must enjoy children.

I believe in firm discipline.

Students are able to approach me and talk to me anywhere in school.

Some teachers do not approve of my being close to students.

I treat students equally to the best of my abilities.

I believe that my presence in the class as a human being is as important as the knowledge I present.

I praise students when they are worthy of praise.

I do not ridicule students.

I do not pretend to be above me class nor do I belittle students.

I attempt to be my real self in the classroom as often as possible.

When appropriate I tell the class how I feel.

When a student dislikes me I do not crumble and become defensive.

When I am displeased with my group I show my anger.

I try to be available to my students outside of classroom time.

I listen to what a student tells me.

I keep students' personal information confidential.

I show empathy to the best of my ability.

Although I realize I can be hurt, I still believe it is necessary to risk.

RESULTS: Notice the accent is on effective interaction in the classroom. The material you teach is equally important. Do you believe that both are important in the classroom? Why? What makes an effective teacher? Does an "A" mean success? Usually a successful teacher is also a successful human being.

SELF-CONCEPT AND ADULTHOOD

Compared with children, adults are ideally more mature, objective, and responsible. Age is not the most important variable in one's life; how one thinks and feels are the crucial factors. You begin by looking at who you are as a person. The first stage in overcoming loneliness is to be content with yourself, a stage that you reach by honest evaluation. When you can live with yourself then you can move to the second stage of developing relationships that are meaningful to you. However, you must remember that living alone is not necessarily a sign of loneliness. Thus again, the emphasis is on the self, how you can change in order to like and accept yourself. This is worth the effort and the time; it is never too late.

What you think of yourself has been affected by events that occurred during childhood. The adult who had positive experiences and feedback, whose successes outnumbered his failures, whose parents and teachers were superior human beings, can cross the threshold of new experiences with some confidence. He is not necessarily assured a rosy existence, because throughout life many variables may affect his self-image. Sometimes he becomes emotionally hurt. After the bruises, comes the long, slow, healing process.

Adulthood involves any number of factors affecting self-concept. I will mention some that I feel are quite significant.

HOW WE SEE OURSELVES

The majority of people are probably better than the image they have of themselves. They often do not perceive themselves as they really are, and they often see others as better than themselves. They can be quite objective with other people, but when they turn to themselves, their perceptions are subjective.

The way we perceive is often affected by our own values and attitudes; we often see only what we want to see. The perception is selective and usually consistent with the self. For example, if you see yourself as a tough guy, you will act in a tough manner. You behave in terms of who you think you are. When you receive information about yourself, you either accept or reject it in terms of how compatible it is with your self-image. Your attitude toward yourself is very central in determining how you are going to behave. Behavior is as variable as people are themselves.

Often our actions are given some form of approval from others. When this happens, we tend to repeat our behavior. The man who sits around and tells dirty jokes while having his beers, sees himself as a bit of a clown, or at least as a good storyteller. People sit around, laugh, and pound the table. The reaction he gets is one of approval; he sees himself as a comic and continues to play this role.

Some of the people I see around me do not perceive themselves in a very accurate manner. I know one person who sees himself as a fairly gifted academic, one who can write and publish. He also sees himself as a successful teacher. I have tried to analyze him as accurately as I possibly could, but my perceptions of him are different from his. To me, he is not what he thinks he is. Thinking you are better than you are is just as bad as thinking you are worse than you are. Both ways of thinking are false, and your self-image suffers in the process.

How can you see yourself more accurately? You obviously must rely on the information that others give you, as well as the information that you receive from yourself. You can make an honest evaluation of yourself if you listen to your feelings. You can do this only if your defenses are virtually nonexistent. Look at your positive and negative characteristics as accurately as you possibly can. How do you react to these characteristics? Can you honestly accept your perceptions? Is it possible to modify or change some of your negative aspects of self? Why? It is extremely important to get some feedback from one or two close friends who can communicate their feelings without being hurt in the process. If you do not have a person who is close to you, then you cannot have a complete picture of yourself. Examine all the pieces of the puzzle, not just those you want to see. Remove your rose-colored glasses and look carefully.

Exercise 6 is related to Exercises 1-3. The incomplete sentences pertain to certain aspects of the self. Complete each sentence as honestly as you can. You may find a couple of surprises.

Exercise 6:
Gaining Self-Insight

AIM: To learn more about how you and others feel about you.

PROCESS: Without being defensive, you are able to take an honest look at different aspects of yourself and learn who you are. We are never really certain. We spend all our lives learning. Complete the sentences with whatever first comes to mind.

I like myself because . . .
I like to . . .
I am most happy when . . .

If I were the leader of a country, I would . . .
I think a good job is . . .
I would like my friends to . . .
If I could spend all my time doing one thing, it would be . . .
The thing I would like people to admire me for is . . .
Something I have never told anyone before is . . .
I really get excited when . . .
I am really good at . . .
In my lifetime I would most like to accomplish . . .
I am . . .
I want to be . . .
I was . . .
I don't want to . . .
I don't like to . . .
I feel important when . . .
I am able to . . .
The best thing about my body is . . .
People enjoy me most when . . .
I feel best when people . . .
I am concerned about . . .
The world would be a better place if . . .
It is not fair that I . . .

RESULTS: What did you learn about yourself? What are your strong points?
What other statements are you able to add to describe yourself?

HOW WE LOOK

One positive asset a person can possess is a good physical appearance. Maybe magazines and television have brainwashed us by showing what we can do with the right cosmetics or the right clothes, but we must agree that attractiveness contributes to a healthy self-image. When I see pictures of Audrey Hepburn, I cannot help but think that a nice appearance is a great gift. However, most of us are not movie stars, and must work at making the most of our appearance. Even though it is only one of the many variables that lead to a positive self-concept, I admit that it is a good beginning.

Having good looks does not mean we are perfect. We can be very attractive and yet be as dull as a doorknob. Intelligence, personality, and a pleasant appearance form a very fortunate combination indeed. In our society the attractive person does receive attention from others. However, we can be fooled by appearance alone. There are many beautiful people who have very little to offer as human begins. A pleasant personality, a good sense of humor, and general friendliness add a great deal to our total image.

Beauty, a sexy body, or a muscle man physique may have their glory during a certain portion of life, but the wise person also develops other areas, such as interpersonal relationships. If you are almost totally concerned with your physical image, you are building a rather shaky foundation for life. You can experience emotional disaster when your sexy look turns to wrinkles and your biceps reflect the gleam of your bald head. We all know of certain movie stars who were devastated after spending all their energy in developing a sexy image. Nothing is left when makeup fails to cover the wrinkles and the hairpiece floats to the floor.

No, appearance does not necessarily rule your life, and to live solely for the purpose of being attractive can lead to a very shallow existence. However, there is no reason why people should not take pride in their appearance. How can you feel good about yourself if you have long, greasy hair, a protruding belly, and a dirty pair of jeans? We have abundant supplies of water; people should at least be able to keep clean. Clothes do not make the man, but they do make you feel better about yourself and they give pleasure to others. I cannot imagine how a person can feel good about himself if he wanders around in garments that look like they had been slept in for a few days. As a rule, if you look well there is a better chance that you will feel well. We have beauty aides that are supposed to help us be gorgeous, but they are not necessarily the answer. The answer lies in proper diet and exercise. A little care for outward appearance is within everyone's reach. Give yourself a boost by putting your best foot forward.

Exercise 7 concerns that brief description of self-concept and appearance. Since we look at ourselves in the mirror everyday, it is important to see exactly what we are looking at. It is true that we do not judge a person solely by his appearance, but we cannot deny its importance.

Exercise 7:
Looking at One's Appearance

AIM: To examine one's physical appearance.

PROCESS: Looking at oneself is not easy. Answer the following statements as they refer to you:

Are you satisified with your basic grooming? What improvement(s) are you able to make?
Do you manage to maintain a fresh look during the day?
Do you wash (bathe) often. Too often?
Are your eating habits satisfactory?
Do you get enough rest?
Do you exercise frequently?
Are you able to cope with worry? Stress?
Do you limit your intake of tobacco and alcohol?
Do your clothes become you?
Do you treat yourself to nice, new clothing once in a while?
Is coordination of clothing important to you? Why?
Do your clothes maintain a fresh, clean look?
Do your clothes reflect *you* rather than trends or fashions?
Do your clothes look cheap?
Do you prefer a lot of ordinary clothes or a few good articles?
Do your shoes match your wardrobe?
Do you remind yourself to walk and sit straight?
What are your strongest physical assets?
What needs attention and improvement?
Are your teeth in good condition?
Do you constantly wish you could have plastic surgery?
Are you overweight?
Does your hairstyle suit you?
Do you care for your skin?
Do you look better when you have a tan?

RESULTS: Granted, we don't all look like movie stars, but are we able to put our best foot forward? Do we think appearance is sometimes, often, or never important? Why? If five equally qualified people apply for a job, who gets it? Why? Change takes effort. Is it worth it?

WORK ATTITUDES

Regardless of what type of work you do, there is a certain amount of satisfaction in doing it successfully. The crowning glory comes when you enjoy what you are doing. Unfortunately most of our success in work is measured in terms of dollars rather than selffulfillment or sheer personal satisfaction. Life is too short to work only for monetary gain. People should realize that they spend a third of their lives at work and striving only for money, with little job satisfaction, is a sad situation. To make matters worse, being unemployed does very little for one's self-image.

An individual who works solely to survive does not enhance his self-worth. Moreover, this is unfortunately often the case in our society. One must work to be able to purchase the means of survival. If this is the only purpose of his work, how can this person grow?

Another sign of our times is the lack of pride that some people take in what they do. For many, work simply means putting in time and picking up a paycheck. With little or no experience, people expect to make thousands. Fortunately, others do show pride in their work. They use what talents they have, regardless of how professional or non-professional the work is. In these situations, one becomes more satisfied with his well-being; his self-worth grows in a positive direction. The total *you* becomes greater than the mere sum of the parts.

In my lifetime, teaching has been my main work. At a very early age, I discovered that farming was not my cup of tea, but I loved to study and teach. I have thoroughly enjoyed my nineteen years of teaching; for me this is the ultimate occupation. Many people would not agree with me, but it is probably true that people work in trades and professions that add very little to their happiness. I think it is necessary to enjoy what one is doing above and beyond the monetary rewards. However, in reality it is not possible to survive beyond Maslow's second level of needs without money. Given unemployment and tight job markets, the artist may turn to making milk shakes and a teacher may be forced to drive a taxi. This is a tragedy in our society. For those who work in their chosen trades and professions, and hate every minute, I can only suggest looking for alternatives. It is never too late to try something which will help fulfill one's needs and enhance self-worth. I have seen people who were able to embark on a new career in middle age. It is worth the risk to change.

Since work is part of our lives and we spend many hours earning our money, Exercise 8 can help us look at what we are doing as well as the positive and negative aspects of our work.

Exercise 8:
Evaluating Your Work

AIM: To re-evaluate the work you are now doing.

PROCESS: Work takes up many hours of our lives. Like other aspects of life, we must take a close look at what we are doing. Formulate several areas of work such as hours, pay, holidays, shift work, role, freedom, administration, your contribution, fulfillment, colleagues, boss, boredom, security, retirement, promotion, and appreciation. Rank them in order of importance to you.

RESULTS: Does your job reflect your rank? What control do you have? Why are some people able to change jobs while others are afraid of change? What control do we have? Why do we complain? Is it always justified? Does a happier home life lead to a happier work life? When does one decide to take action? Do we have control over our lives? Why are only some able to take risks? At what point does your health enter the picture?

GETTING ALONG WITH OTHERS

Since man is a social animal, many of his waking hours are spent in human interaction. We are angry with, pity, or avoid the person who cannot work with other coworkers, who is forever complaining, or who is always fighting or behaving miserably. Such people can use all the defense mechanisms they wish but often experience loneliness.

Every role such as parent, grandparent, spouse, friend, or acquaintance has special characteristics which make it meaningful. To fail as a husband or father is undoubtedly a traumatic experience. Regardless of how much blame you place on the other person, you look at yourself and realize that you are responsible for at least part of the failure. If the role was an important one in your life, failures in this area can damage your self-image to the point where you feel life is not worthwhile. It is understandable why some people will not take risks and use all their defense mechanisms to protect their sense of worth, as slight as it may be.

Having some degree of success in a relationship can enable a person to look at himself in an honest, positive way. Such a person

158

may not necessarily be totally happy with himself, but can probably reach out to other people without hiding behind his shell. We admire a person who is confident, who can hold his head high, and face the world. When we do not admire such a person, it is only because we see in him something we wish for ourselves. Not everyone is happy to see a successful person.

It is necessary to look at one's relationships in terms of needs, expectations, and fulfillment. As usual, life goes on and many people do not take time out to examine their immediate environment. Sometimes their attitude is to grin and bear it. Listen to your feelings and attempt to hear what they are trying to tell you. Of course, it is difficult to sit down and look at what is happening because often the truth hurts. However, you do very little for yourself if you continue the same behavior patterns. You simply continue to exist inside your lonely shell.

Furthermore, it is necessary to look at your values and your attitudes. Do you truly enjoy interacting with a group of thirty people? Would you rather be by yourself in the evening? Do you go to a gathering merely because you feel that it is an obligation, but deep down inside do not enjoy yourself? What is your relationship with your friends or with your spouse? Is it as good as it should be? Why? Are you able to communicate your feelings? These are very difficult questions to answer but necessary if you are to engage in meaningful relationships. Otherwise you suffer in silence.

Exercise 9 enables us to focus briefly on some of our relationships. Sometimes we take relationships for granted and sometimes we blame other people. If there is something negative in a relationship, we should think of areas that need improvement.

Exercise 9:
Relationships

AIM: To examine some of the positive and negative aspects of your relationships with various individuals.

PROCESS: Look at yourself in terms of your relationships with some of the following: spouse, children, siblings, parents, close relatives, friends, acquaintances, colleagues. List some of the positive and negative aspects and how/where a relationship can be improved.

RESULTS: What are your priorities in relationships? Do they change? Why? Are you more comfortable with closeness? Distance? Are you honest with your excuses? Do you do things to please others instead of yourself? Should relatives be friends? Where do you draw the line in socializing?

HOW WE CAN CHANGE

Time and time again we hear that people do not change, thus we must either accept or reject them as they are. Others feel they can change another person or at least influence their behavior. Although there may be some truth in these statements, they are not totally accurate. People can, and do, change. They do not change their height or some aspects of their basic personality, but they can and do change their attitudes, which in turn affect their behavior. Some people do not want to change. They are happy in their environment of self-pity and narrow survival. They appear on this earth to suffer and reap rewards afterwards. Some people study psychology and know all the theories, but when it comes to self, they are too oblivious to attempt anything constructive. Some can understand the behavior of others but not their own. Change involves a desire to change and constant effort; it does not happen automatically.

If you want to understand others, probe within yourself. We have heard time and time again the exhortation "know thy self" but how seldom people listen to these words. They are too busy gossiping and enjoying juicy stories about others (preferably negative) to take the time to examine themselves. Some feel they don't have to look at themselves; others are afraid, in case they find something they do not wish to see.

What can you do? First, you must be honest with yourself. During some of your quiet moments reflect on your present state. Be as objective with yourself as you are with other people even if you are used to playing roles and wearing masks. You have been taught not to show your feelings. "Don't be a baby!" seems to ring in your mind. You learned to bottle up your feelings, to share less, and cope on your own. You often do not know who you are and do not want others to know either. Now is the time for change.

Show yourself to other people; show your attitudes and feelings. This is not easy to do. You see, if I am honest with you, then you will tend to be more honest with me. The cycle is repeated. In addition, there is some risk involved, but this is how you grow. If you are honest, then you get honest feedback. Even children know when a person is a phony and when he is honest. A phony will tell you what you want to hear and not what he really feels. Where there is more openness, there is more freedom in interpersonal interactions and there is more learning about self.

You must learn to listen. You must listen not only to the words the person is saying, but to what he is feeling and what he is perceiving. Often when a person is speaking we are busy trying to interrupt or, at least, politely wait for our turn, anxious to spew out our little bits of wisdom. Even if you are listening, you are usually making judgments and assumptions as to what the person is saying and feeling. Sometimes you only hear what you want to hear and sometimes you think you hear what is said. You must accept the fact that what the person says is real to him, even though you may disagree.

The poor listener is the person who is very much involved with himself. He feels so important that it is not worth his effort to exert himself to pay attention. I think that the person who talks a great deal usually does not have that much to say; in fact, he is controlling the situation and thus protecting himself from the risk of having to change, if only a point of view. Talk less and listen more.

Accept yourself. You are still unique with all your positive and negative characteristics. If you honestly think well of yourself, then you may think well of others. On the other hand, if you are a disapproving person, you probably disapprove of yourself and others. Listen to your heart; listen to your ideas and emotions. See who you are and who you would like to be. New Year's resolutions are not the answer. Examine feedback that you receive, not only from friends but from other people as well. At times we must have our point of view challenged, and our ideas and attitudes evaluated. Probably our best friends can knock us down and pick us up again without any loss of friendship. If the responses you get are mainly negative and you proceed to walk on clouds as if you are the greatest, then you have a long way to go. Clouds may not give you too much support. It is bad enough to have your head in the clouds, let alone feet. The visibility is rather limited.

Spend some time alone. Use your time constructively by think-

ing instead of worrying. With an honest assessment of yourself, you
will soon realize that you can change your life and live it pretty well
as you wish. However, simply saying things to yourself is not the
answer. "I am going to enjoy my own company," or "I think I can do
it if I try," will not solve the problem. You need mental discipline.
Our great people didn't reach their levels of accomplishment by
sitting around and wishing. They wanted to do something; they
wanted to be *somebody*. So, start with some small task, like reading
one chapter in a book. It is important to complete the task because if
you do not, you will only hate yourself more. You want to be able to
depend on yourself. With this accomplishment, you will feel some
degree of happiness and a corresponding decrease of loneliness.

There is no point in feeling sorry for yourself. If you are an
honest person, you will not fool yourself. If you think you need
help, ask for it; there is no crime or shame in asking for the assistance
of others. If at all possible, smile, for it radiates warmth not only to
yourself but to others as well. On the other hand, if you want to cry,
let the tears flow. Laughing and crying are both essential to your
mental health.

What happens if you do not listen and accept? You continue
your way along the bumpy road of life with all your defense
mechanisms at your control. You blame the world and not yourself.
You are not born inferior to others; you learn to act that way. If you
blame everyone for your attitude and overreact to what people say,
you begin to feel persecuted. Your head begins to droop. Loneliness
knocks on your door.

Loneliness I deals with self-concept. If you feel good about
yourself, Loneliness I decreases. Exercise 10 deals with questions
that relate to a healthy, positive self-image.

Exercise 10:
Healthy Self-Concepts

AIM: To examine the development of self-concept.

PROCESS: See if the following statements apply to you:

I am a valuable person.
People find me interesting.
I am able to express my feelings.

I enjoy doing many things.
I enjoy being idle sometimes.
I need other people, but not to build myself up at their expense.
I feel I am productive in my work.
I do not allow people to rule me.
I make the best possible decisions.
I do not blame the world for my mistakes.
I am human and therefore not perfect.
I have both success and failure in my life.
I learn from my mistakes.
I feel equal to people around me.
I am able to accept both praise and constructive criticism from others.
I realize that worrying does not lead to progress.
I change my values as I grow.
I have a philosophy of life.
I listen to others.
I like myself.
I am honest with myself and others.

RESULTS: Positive responses indicate positive development and growth.

We will never reach a point in our lives when we can claim to be perfect. We are taking the human journey whose origin is birth and destination is death. We have very little control over an invisible force that moves so swiftly down the road. Although we are unable to deal with this invisible force, we are capable of making the trip more enjoyable, since we have no chance to make U-turns along the way. Some travel first class and others crawl. We comfort ourselves by saying, "There are some who are better off than I, but there are many who are worse off. Why should I complain or worry?" Maybe it's all right to be stuck somewhere in the middle with the masses. I do not agree.

Along the human journey, we occasionally pause to rest, think, listen to our heartbeat, and dream. With a smile on our faces, our body tingles with brief excitement; we inhale deeply, then feel relaxation overtake us. We are content because we have grown as individuals; we are honestly happy with ourselves. But happiness knows no bounds. We move outward, beyond ourselves, reaching toward others. Loneliness is seeking new friends; we find others who have left the silent company. We cannot stop now.

nine
Overcoming Loneliness II: Achieving Relationships

How can we reach out to others? Relationships do not simply form out of the blue. For most of us it takes effort to reach out, not to many, but only to a selected few. Somehow, reaching out makes life a little more complete and worthwhile. We need someone we can respect, accept, and trust. In marriage our spouse should be the very best friend we have. Achieving this type of relationship can be a great experience for both partners. We need to be cared for and wanted; we need a place in someone's mind and heart. If we can reach this zenith in life, we can be assured that loneliness will not follow in our steps.

INITIATING RELATIONSHIPS

At times we feel that we do not want to get involved in any serious relationships. We are content to be responsible only to ourselves rather than to some other person or persons. This is especially true when we experience a rotten day at work, an unhappy experience involving others, or when we do not feel well. Sometimes when we look over our fence or balcony, we are not impressed with what we see. How do we decide what to do?

There is a lot of truth in the idea that people and their actions often impede our struggle for survival. How often we hurt each other! How foolish to experience the games people play! How narrow and rigid we are in our perceptions! And yet, despite this human chaos, we must realize that people can also represent hope. Regardless of what we see across the fence or between the walls, we are aware that it is possible to share with another person. We can be special and different from others.

To be or not to be in a relationship is a decision that only we can make. At least we do have the choice regardless of the emotional dilemma we experience. If we set our goal in the direction of searching for a relationship with considerable determination, we can end our journey with disappointment. When we keep our options open, we at least give ourselves a chance to experience surprise. As I have mentioned previously, if you are confident, feel worthwhile, and have experienced growth, then you are able to put yourself in a position where relationships are possible.

A relationship does not mean that you have a good time or a casual encounter with someone. It represents a closeness, an intimacy with another person. We care, but we are cared for as well; we share our feelings in depth. Neither partner is boss or subordinate; the union is totally mutual. How can we refuse a relationship of this nature? We are able to restore our faith in the worth and beauty of our species.

In a meaningful relationship we change and grow. We never feel that we have reached a plateau where we can remain unchanged for the rest of our lives. We continue to feel the presence of another person, his closeness and sensitivity, but we also remain individuals. Being open to the other individual does not entail any feelings of guilt or fear. Feelings are reciprocal; love thrives in this atmosphere.

In order to reach out I think that it is necessary to risk. Risking is not the same for all people. It depends on the type of person you are and especially on how you see yourself. For one individual, taking a risk can be child's play; for another, a risk may mean hours and days of frustration and agony. Whatever the case may be, we take risks because we do not know what the outcome will be. Our ego is involved, but we are not certain if the net result will be some form of humiliation, shame, or rejection. Even the student who puts his hand up to answer a question, is taking a risk. For an adult it may involve changing professions at fifty years of age, or seeking a new mate. There are always degrees of emotional involvement associated with risk taking.

Most of us have experienced some degree of risk in relationships and the accompanying acceptance or rejection from others. If I risk by reaching out to someone and there is acceptance, then my self-concept grows. On the other hand, when I am rejected, my self-concept responds to my feelings and often shrinks. But what do I gain if I do not risk? I experience isolation, freedom from hurt, and my self remains more of a mystery to me. I can only imagine who I am, with all my strengths and weaknesses.

Reaching out and risking can also involve the defense mechanisms. One may reach out for a selfish motive. He wishes to gain at the expense of the other person, to gain only for himself without concern for the other; he may achieve this by reaching out when the other person is emotionally vulnerable. People hate to be used by others, but it is amazing to see this game frequently played. For some, reaching out is easier when they reach toward wealth, status, fame, or beauty. Both sexes are guilty of reaching out just for the thrill or fun of it all. There is no problem when both of the individuals are totally aware of what is going on. Unfortunately, one often wears a mask in some of these situations and continues to dream that everything is going to be just perfect.

Sometimes we reach out for reasons other than the mere relationship itself. For one person, the challenge and the attention that he receives from others is all that interests him. The person at the other end is merely an object. Imagine a man who bets that he can pick up or date an attractive girl. The girl is only of secondary importance to him; the challenge is what really counts. If both are aware that they are playing a game, then nobody wins or loses. If one is hurt in the process then it can no longer be called a game. Once the mountain has been conquered, the person moves on to new and more exciting peaks in an endless range. For some, life certainly is fun and games.

Although at one time or another most of us like to indulge in a bit of daydreaming, it is very important for us to be as realistic as possible. It is amazing how some people will cling to fantasy, dreams, and hopes. Some believe in total luck and wait around for a miracle to happen. Somehow life goes on, and the painful questions never seem to rise to the level of consciousness. Some are afraid to ask or to look. An acquaintance of mine recently talked about one of his friends who is a university graduate in business, and an alcoholic as well. His girlfriend is afraid to lose him and keeps hoping for the best. She gives him her credit card, and while she works or sits at home, he entertains some of his friends to the tune of one hundred dollars per evening. My acquaintanace related how this man laughed out loud describing how the night before he had drunk cognac at her expense. I wonder what goes through the girlfriend's mind when she subjects herself to such utter nonsense.

The idea of falling in love is very much an individual matter. It may take time and work, yet no two people will be similar to two others. Two people may meet and become instant friends; the same can hold for true love relationships. Probably there is very little difference. After all, love is friendship, or put in other words, two people in love are the best of friends.

It is interesting how the human journey leads one through the colorful countryside of life. The fun part is that we are never certain what lies around the next turn. True, there is a possibility of encountering a great deal of sadness, but that is the mystery of life. Thus I am a great believer in chance with all the risk taking associated with it. Even though at times you may be quite certain of the outcome, there is still an element of surprise. From my own experience, some of the most beautiful people I have as close friends were bumped into by chance. I do not know what force puts one in the right place at the right time. Maybe this is the definition of luck. Whatever it is, some people are lucky enough to be there at the right time. Others, less fortunate, aren't even there at the wrong time.

However, common interests and certain human qualities that people see in each other also create a closer bind between them. If you are a person who likes humor, intelligent conversation, and a wholesome disposition, then you will be attracted to the person who displays those qualities. How wonderful it is when two people appreciate each other for the qualities that they admire in each other.

People are human and they have mutual needs. I want a person whom I can love and who can love me in return. I want someone who can say positive things about my behavior and about me as a person. I want a true friend to treat me as a unique person. I want someone to share my thoughts and feelings, my happy and sad moments, someone to laugh and cry with. In other words, I want a person to share my life.

As has been stressed before, the clue lies in knowing who you are. When we know ourselves we can begin to know what and who we want. In other words Loneliness II can be conquered after the defeat of Loneliness I.

And yet how often we tend to seek friends or mates for reasons that would cause wise men to slowly shake their heads. Men so often want someone to take care of them. They want a surrogate mother with a few more additives. With male chauvanism (some call it sexism) still rather rampant in our society, men are not supposed to be able to look after themselves. They cannot cook a good stew, clean out the refrigerator, iron their apron, or clean the toilet bowl. Many consider that their mate's only job is to look after the home and them.

Some men feel a great need to have a mate to look after. Like some females who never feel they are women unless they have a child, there are men who think they will never be male unless they have a woman by their side. There is merit in having a good friend but not if that person is as dependent as an orphaned child. There are many types of relationships. Recently I heard of an eighty-year-old man wanting to marry a high school girl. Maybe the girl wants someone to look after her. Either way, we should each look after ourselves first before we worry about looking after others.

I would not advise any man to work on a relationship which is based on pity. I have yet to see one healthy relationship where one or both partners feel sorry for each other and simply stick together. The underlying factor seems to involve the concept of change. A man who feels sorry for a girl for one reason or another thinks that she will change when they marry. However, this is wishful thinking. Look at Bob. He married Martha who was already pregnant by another man. She told him she didn't know where to go or what to do. He felt sorry for her but is now more sore than sorry. Martha gave him his walking papers, because she recently traded him in for a new, younger model.

The same holds true for sex. There are many men who feel they simply cannot exist another day without sex. This obsession is as neurotic as overeating. Many males think that a female at their side entitles them to intercourse at the snap of their fingers. They are insensitive to or misinformed about their partner's feelings, because many men are certain that all women need and want sex as well.

Rather than accepting the attitude that sex is a necessary drive for survival or that sex stops heart attacks, one should think of sex as a private, intimate form of communication. Sex does fulfill the human need to be physically close. When two people care for each other, as they should in a good relationship, the closeness that sex provides adds to the overall friendship. Since touching is an important human need, sex provides for this need, but should not be a substitute for touching.

Many people still feel a stigma is attached to touching, and that it is not permissible. I remember how students used to love being touched. You could see it written all over their faces and yet many would pretend to draw away and be embarrassed when it happened. All of us love to be touched. We thrive on it, but only when someone meaningful does the touching. Sex simply enhances the touching.

Sex may be a substitute for love and attention but only in meaningful relationships does it enhance the two needs. We are only human, and thus we love attention from others. However, I doubt that many women really get a thrill from men who yell and whistle at them from their trucks or cars. I think that the majority of women do enjoy love and attention, but only from the right person. Attention can be given by many people who are important to you; however, love comes from only a selected group of close friends.

Loneliness II relates to relationships. When we are able to have a close friend, we are able to experience a richer life. Exercise 11 allows us to examine some of the reasons for initiating relationships. Only we can decide if the answers we give ourselves are meaingful or not.

Exercise 11:
Initiating Relationships

AIM: To examine ourselves in terms of initiating relationships.

PROCESS: Since relationships are a serious matter, it is necessary to examine ourselves in terms of our needs and purposes. Examine the following reasons for seeking a relationship, and determine how important they are to you.

Pressure from parents.
Pressure from others.
Need for a companion for social functions.
Desire to marry.
Need a companion for sport functions.
Age.
Financial sharing.
"Left out" feeling.
Friends are all married.
Going steady means stability.
It's the normal thing to do.
Sexual desires.
Need to love and be loved.
Desire to settle down and raise children.
More purpose in life.

RESULTS: Are your actions and thoughts similar? Are you doing what you want to do? Are you trying to please others?

MEETING PEOPLE

Although we are constantly among people, meeting someone who truly interests us is no easy task. Our society has taken the problem to heart. We can see the emergence of singles clubs, ladies' nights, bars, discos, singles apartments, and cruises for the unattached. We must agree that the desire to meet the right person and the success rate do not consistently coincide. Meeting people is no problem, but meeting the right person is like seeking hidden treasure. "Seek and ye shall find" does not apply to scores of people.

Thus even before beginning a relationship it is necessary to start with yourself, to be happy with who you are, and to be honest with your feelings, because the only person you fool is yourself. I honestly believe it is possible to try *too* hard. I may be superstitious, but it seems that the harder you seek, the more you want someone, the more difficult it is to achieve your goal. You seem to end up with nothing. Trying too hard is not the answer.

Of course you do not sit in front of the television set and wait for Mr. Right to knock on your door, or expect to come home and find a price or princess in your bed waiting for you. To begin with, you must please yourself first. Do not dress for other people; dress for youself. Show off what you have; think of yourself as someone special. This is how other people will see you as well. Organize your life, and do not let chaos be a part of your repertoire of behavior. Life and living are beautiful. Smile.

As previously mentioned, one of the most important characteristics you should have is confidence. In fact, this attribute is more important to you than all the money in the bank. Your confidence can sometimes be perceived as a threat by the opposite sex, and some members of the same sex may hate or envy you. Remember, the problem is theirs not yours. It is important not to dwell on the past. Even if your loved one ran away a month ago, that is no reason why you should sit back and perceive yourself as a total failure. Of course, introspection is necessary, but it seems unreasonable that you should carry all the guilt and blame on your shoulder. You could fall victim to insecurity.

If you require a period of time to tie your thoughts together, to know who you really are, then by all means focus your attention on number one. This could take a great deal of effort and time. It is a wise and necessary plan of action to follow. If you jump into a new relationship when you are not ready, Loneliness I and II will be your constant companions. However, it is unnecessary to dwell only on the negative aspects of your life. Why spend your time thinking that only the worst can happen? Give yourself a break. Think of all your positive attributes even for only a few moments.

Unless you are out for an evening of bright lights and thrills, I would recommend that you avoid high-risk places for meeting people. Bars would fall into this category. If you enjoy these places, then you must be aware of what you are doing and what your intentions are. Don't complain about the aftermath and tell yourself you should have known better. In high-risk places you encounter a great deal of fast talk, smoothness, and high pressure salesmanship if you are a female. Of course, there is no reason why a girl cannot provide the pressure as well. In these situations, your brain can become rattled and you may fall victim to the hungry wolf. Don't be surprised if you lose your head as well as your picnic basket in the process!

We would be much wiser to reach out to people when we are relaxed. Places of work, sports, classes, social gatherings, or any number of situations where we are involved in social interaction are low-risk spots. The pace is less hectic, and we have more time to think and thus less chance to get rattled. An individual knows the people at work somewhat better than someone in the changing bar scene. If you are asked out to dinner and you do not wish to accept, you have time to express your feelings. I have heard people give reasons such as "I'm busy on Friday," "I'm leaving for Paris on Sunday," or "I'm too busy with housework." All of these replies are usually alibies. Why not give a straight, honest answer? Mind you, humans often do not hear anyway.

You are more relaxed while engaging in forms of activity other than parties where you are holding a cocktail glass or making superficial conversation. On the other hand, it is foolish to be always in the middle of frantic activity. The more calm and collected your actions, the clearer your thinking and perception. It is best to see the world through your contact lenses rather than rose-colored glasses. Part of the relaxed state is also being your natural self. I wonder why we must try to impress or at least make our presence noticeable to others. I wonder if we sometimes confuse a person's confidence with being a snob. There is something very appealing about a person who looks and acts naturally.

First impressions are lasting. When I meet people for the first time, I look at them very closely. I especially notice the level or depth of the person's thoughts. It is always wise to talk less and listen more. It is interesting to note if the thoughts originate mainly in the head, heart, or genital area. If, after a few minutes of conversation, someone asks you to spend the weekend with them so they can get to know you better, you should have a fair idea where that thought originates.

Let us presume that you have initiated a relationship and in your quiet moments wonder if you are doing the right thing. If you are honest with your feelings, then you have a pretty good idea about the quality of your interaction. However, there are several other factors that are worth considering when you meet people.

One should feel neither superior nor inferior to the other in a good relationship. The key is equality. Why should there be one boss? What is wrong with two heads? Unless they live in a caste system, people who feel equal usually have similar backgrounds. Education, type of work, and salary are usually relevant in relationships. Maybe a college graduate should not feel superior to an eighth grade dropout. However, differences can be marked. Similar backgrounds, values, interests, and perceptions contribute to the equal sign among people.

What has happened to trust in our society? Why is there a great deal of energy lost in worrying about a partner fooling around? I recall that on more than one occasion before going overseas on business, friends began worrying about my behavior away from home. The prevailing question is how can a female be expected to remain at home and not be tempted by all the macho wolves and coyotes? How much late night window shopping can I really do in Soho? I wonder if trust really exists when I see so many men and women looking through their partners in search of someone who might at least temporarily increase the flow of adrenalin. Maybe we can make a profitable business from the sale of chastity belts, yet in a good relationship trust should be unquestioned. If two people love, respect, and care for each other, they may look but have no need to touch others. If a relationship grows without trust, vows or contracts are not the answer.

Absence may not make the heart grow fonder, but physical presence does not keep people together either. Quality is more important than quantity in good relationships. I would agree that togetherness is pleasant when people are fond of each other; however, there is no need to breathe down each other's necks. Sometimes months and years pass by without seeing a dear friend. When you meet, it seems that time stood still. You begin where you last left off. There is so much to talk about and so many ideas to share. Obviously there is depth in the quality of the relationship. If you meet a friend and after "Hello," or "How are you?" you are stuck for words, your next remark should be "Goodbye."

Two people who are fond of each other should be relaxed in their relationship. There is no need to impress or worry about perfection. We often hear one person spending half his time apologizing for his shortcomings. If you are constantly insecure, and you find stressful solutions constantly interfering with your encounters, then your relationship is far from ideal. If I am fond of you, why must you worry about having snails or frog's legs to feed me when I am hungry? What happened to the hot dog? I would rather eat beans from a paper plate with someone I care for than caviar from a gold plate with a person who is not relevant or meaningful in my life.

Individuals in a relationship should feel comfortable with each other. There should be little concern for entertaining or being entertained. Silence can be as precious as constant chattering. To begin with, you should enjoy your own company and be perfectly happy to be by yourself as well. It is not necessary to blow kisses at each other to prove your love. The eyes often speak for themselves. If you have to wind yourself up each time you are in a relationship, then it is time to throw away the key.

Statements in Exercise 12 ask you and your partner to look at the quality of relationship you have. Your responses can enable you to determine the areas of similarities and differences between you.

Exercise 12:
Looking at Yourself and Your Partner

AIM: To evaluate your relationship.

PROCESS: Answer the following questions first as they apply to you and then as they apply to your partner. Simply substitute "he/she" for "I" when looking at your partner.

I am able to express my love both physically and verbally.
I listen to my partner, to both the words and the feelings the words express.
I am able to accept love from my partner.
I have compete trust in my partner.
I communicate to my partner all my business transactions.
I communicate to my partner feelings of anger and fear as well as happiness and excitement.
I am able to honestly clarify my goals in life to my partner.
To the best of my ability, I do not use defense mechanisms with my partner.
I am sensitive to the goals and aspirations of my partner.
I try to be sensitive to my partner's emotions.
I want my partner to openly communicate his/her feelings in my presence.

I desire that my partner be an individual who is not totally dependent on me.

I would rather be with my partner than with any other person during my spare time.

I enjoy sharing chores with my partner.

I am not using my partner selfishly.

I honestly respect my partner as a unique human being.

I am honestly committed to my relationship.

I reinforce my partner frequently.

I enjoy intimacy with my partner.

Instead of excuses, I communicate with total honesty.

I have many interests in common with my partner.

RESULTS: What did you learn about yourself? Your partner? Are there more similarities than differences? What areas need improvement?

STAGES IN THE DEVELOPMENT OF A RELATIONSHIP

From their birth to maturity relationships appear to have cycles which are somewhat similar to the life cycles and loneliness previously discussed. Often there are hurdles to overcome when individuals spend some length of time together. If the differences are not resolved, people break their friendship and go separate ways. Sometimes this is a very quick, but not a happy situation. If a relationship begins in an open, honest manner, then it stands a better chance to overcome some of the problems that can arise. The net result can be a beautiful, lasting experience.

The first stage in a relationship is falling in love. What fantastic chemistry one finds in the love machine! Love can grow slowly or grow very quickly, clouding your eyes and completely burying your perceptions in stardust. One experiences feelings of passion, excitement, and acceptance mixed with a few anxieties and fears of rejection. Defenses are lowered, yet there is a fear of total risk. Initially there may be concern about revealing your intelligence, sexual needs and abilities, and even the big mole on your left thigh.

Because you trust, you achieve closeness with another person. The experience can be exhilarating, because you feel someone cherishes and comforts you. To make certain that you do not let each other down, you are both on your best behavior. Your manners are polite, you are extra clean, and your clothes more neatly pressed than ever. Yes, love is truly a beautiful experience. I only wish more of us were successful in keeping it around for a long time.

The second phase of relationships is marked with stress. You realize that differences exist. Since some problems were not discussed during the romantic stage, they begin to surface now. Sometimes you feel you are not contributing to the welfare of each other. Each of you feels like a burden rather than a caring partner. During this stage, individuals begin to be concerned more and more with self. They feel trapped. Often minds spin after nagging or arguing sessions. Couples look at each other, and with a lost look and forced grin on their faces, mumble to themselves, "How did I ever deserve this?"

Problems appear blown out of proportion. Each person blames the other during verbal exchange. Somehow there is very little meeting of minds at this point. "Let's talk about it," you say. "Let's forget it!" says the other. One partner may want to feel some warmth and closeness; the other stomps out the door. With frequent ups and downs, the relationship appears to be headed toward certain failure. If neither individual is willing to communicate, compromise, or show genuine concern, then love slowly begins to dim and flicker. However, there is always hope for some change; often it happens.

The third stage appears to lead to a more mature, less romantic form of relationship. Two people begin to accept themselves and each other more honestly than before. As a result of the emotional upheavals, they focus on the good points of their relationship. All is not lost. During this stage they rely more on each other and become more sensitive to each other's needs. Instead of fighting, they discuss problems as they arise. They trust and respect each other. They experience dependence but also enjoy their autonomy. Love and peace settle over the relationship. The key to success is not luck, but concern and effort.

Finally, the relationship reaches a stage where the individuals can give of themselves to others. The ability to give is a beautiful occurrence. This stage is a form of self-actualized relationship. Because couples do not play games, fight, argue, or constantly worry, they can use the energy toward constructive purposes. Individuals contribute to their work, to each other, and to close friends. What a beautiful goal to strive for!

Exercise 13 allows you to pause and examine at what stage you may be in your relationship.

Exercise 13:
Phases in Relationships

AIM: To be aware of certain stages found in a relationship.

PROCESS: Review your particular relationship in terms of the stages described in this book. Do you recognize any stage that you have experienced in your relationship? What is your present stage? Are both individuals responsible for the occurrence of a stage? Do stages repeat themselves?

MAINTAINING A RELATIONSHIP

Sometimes we are told not to take life seriously. We are not indispensable; the world will rotate with or without us. However, I do not think the same analogy holds true for relationships. The role one plays is important for the welfare of both individuals involved. There is no magic formula; I am not able to give anyone recipes for a happy life. However, lasting, happy relationships must have several characteristics in common.

Similar Interests

In a good relationship both partners should have a fair amount in common. I think it is very difficult to change a person's life style and general interests. If one person spends all his time at work and bird watching, he may find some difficulty in relating to a friend who enjoys cooking and sleeping. It is next to impossible to find two people totally alike, but some major interests should be mutual. It is not true that any person is better than no person at all. Opposites may attract, but people who are similar stay together.

Tolerance

A certain degree of patience and tolerance are necessary in any relationship. Sometimes it is very difficult to sit and wait in the kitchen while your mate has barely started her makeup or wild search for the right pantyhose. Of course, there exist primadonnas who move as if the world had stood still for the last few years. At times I find myself demanding that the next person move as quickly as I do or keep pace with my fast eating. I must be conscious of my demands. None of us are perfect, and in any relationship there is always something that may not be high on the other's list of priorities.

Yet I wonder why some people are as tolerant as they are. The other day I went up to our coffee shop to have a bowl of soup and a sandwich. One of the men who sat next to me ate with his mouth wide open. In fact, his mouth looked and sounded like a cement mixer. I feel certain that he is not aware of this habit, and yet people, myself included, say nothing and the act goes on day after day. Naturally, I would want to say something if the individual were one of my close friends. I cannot see myself moving over to somebody in a restaurant and telling them to stop slurping. I could end up in a fight.

All of us need some practice in respecting the other person's feelings. That is, it is necessary to be able to step into the other person's shoes and identify with his feelings. Most of us know that it is easier to dish out criticism than to give praise. I think that we are protecting ourselves when we do not practice empathy. I remember being very angry with one of my twelfth grade students. When I was attempting an explanation, her mind seemed to be somewhere in the clouds. Little did I know that the girl's mother was extremely ill, and the girl was worried and depressed. Of course I felt like a heel! How often we fly off the handle and criticize another person without too much regard for his welfare. We sometimes use cutting words, downgrading statements, or total indifference. We leave the other person emotionally limp. Do we stop and think how they may be feeling? Of course not! Some aspects of life are like one big cartoon.

Value Clarification

As I have mentioned before, it is necessary to pause in our busy lives and make a checklist which relates specifically to our feelings, our behavior, and our happiness. For example, you might ask yourself questions such as: Do people like me? Do I complain a lot? Do I have many physical ailments? Am I happy with my work? Do I like myself? Do I often feel lonely? Am I a lonely person? Can I do something about my environment? Are my friends actually only acquaintances? Am I happy being alone most of the time? Are my relationships good or are they simply convenient? How honest am I in a relationship? Do people understand me or do they see me as quite different from the person I really am?

Often when we stop and ask ourselves questions, we are in the realm of value clarification. We want to know what is important to us in our daily lives. As a matter of fact, people do not look at their values often enough; others do not even attempt to discover what they want in life. When we value something, we have several alternatives to choose from. We carefully consider what the consequences of each alternative are and decide on the basis of what we feel is the best for us. Once we make a decision about a certain value, we tend to uphold our stand. However, your values do not exist in total isolation from other factors that affect your behavior. Your attitudes also reflect your values, as well as your goals and desires for the present and future. What you most often worry about, what you argue for, and what interests you all reflect your values.

We are often caught in a no man's land because we are faced with the problem of what we would like to be and what we are as individuals. Usually what we are is in part already determined for us by our culture. Parents play a large part in determining what values are instilled in their children. Thus for an adult, a great deal of will power and desire is required to look at not only what values he cherishes but what values he would like to change.

There is no good, bad, or right in terms of the values in a

relationship. You decide what you value. If you have been brain-washed that it is better to be in any kind of relationship rather than no relationship at all, and you truly believe and value this, then it is right for you. The problem arises when you think and feel differently. Remember that the more you accuse other people and blame the entire world for your predicament, the more you are in the world of defense mechanisms. You spend your energy giving reasons and excuses to other people. They turn their ears to the wind when they see you approach. No one wins in this situation.

You need space as an individual in order to keep growing. Life ceases when you are no longer striving, setting new goals, and reaching for greater heights. We respect attitudes and value changes in ourselves and in each other. We contribute to each other's existence, and we are also happy to see each other with plenty of room to breathe.

We must continue to seek and enjoy privacy. In a world filled with schedules and appointments, it is necessary for us to seek some solitude. We must set aside time for some aloneness, for it just does not happen. The frequency and duration is an individual matter. The idea is simply to enjoy the peace and tranquility as a moment when the world stops rushing before your eyes.

Communication

Communication is probably the most important characteristic of any good relationship. Talk for talk's sake is not enough. We must listen not only to the words of the other person but also to the feelings associated with the words. When we wish to convey our pleasure to another person, it seems that words and grammar take care of themselves. When we want to communicate displeasure, we usually express our feelings in terms of *you* statements. "You make me so angry when you say that!" or "You really upset me!" or even "You idiot!" are all examples of *you* statements. Communication is greatly improved when we change *You* to *I*. The expressions would change to "I become so angry when I hear those words!" and "I really feel upset!" The *I* statements do not convey any rejection. The message is not a global one. I am upset with what you are saying or doing, but that does not mean I reject you as a person.

Trust, Commitment,
Spending Time Together

Trust must continue to exist if individuals are to grow in a relationship. I do not think that it is possible to tell people to trust you. Like respect, it comes as a by-product of a healthy partnership. Your actions rather than your words convey trust. A lack of trust leads to insecurity which can further lead to anxiety. These are characteristics to be avoided.

A dynamic relationship requires responsibility and an emotional commitment from us. Of course it is necessary to pay the bills, to work, and to provide for basic physical and security needs. This is not enough. We must give of ourselves emotionally. We continue to give and to receive affection. We need approval from others to feel we are worthwhile individuals.

Two people should continue to spend time together. I am surprised to see how many couples prefer to have other couples travel with them. There is safety in this process because you do not have to relate to one other person all the time. This can be fun occasionally. However, if two people cannot spend time together and enjoy each other's company, then it tells you something about the relationship. On the other hand, if you have not tried being alone together, I highly recommend it. You know, you might really like it.

THE IMPORTANCE
OF RELATIONSHIPS

Because no four people are alike, no two relationships are identical. Often people say that if it works, that's what counts. I do not like this idea because it reminds me of a person using common sense. Killing can be a form of common sense for a psychopath. Likewise, two people can constantly hurt each other and yet maintain a relationship which I would call existence.

Thus, whether we like it or not, we must be able to get along with other people, otherwise we may suffer a loss of relationships which leads to loneliness. We need relationships for our own happiness and effectiveness. This means that it is necessary to learn to love more than to hate. There is no easy recipe, change does not come easily, but I think it is worth the try. If we do not help ourselves and if we do not reach out, we remain lonely people. We continue to bounce off each other like billiard balls on a table. Life is short, and we can fill the space with gold or with straw. I think it is worth striving for the gold. After all, we are all precious material and each of us deserves the best. Do not give up and tarnish with age. Let us attempt to make this world a less lonely place for ourselves as well as for others, for there is joy and beauty in healthy relationships. The peace and humanity surpasses anything that can be found in this world. Anyone in this position is indeed a very fortunate individual. The silent company remains in the far distance and seeks new friends.

When we have a meaningful relationship, we want it to last and grow. Since we grow as human beings, we frequently want to look at our present relationship. The purpose of Exercise 14 is to examine what you like and what you dislike in your relationship. This knowledge can reveal what areas need improvement. In all relationships we must find time simply to listen to our partner without interference. Exercise 15 focuses on the importance of passive listening. However, simply listening is not enough. We must listen to the feelings conveyed by the words. We hear words but that is not enough. We require practice for active listening. Exercise 16 lets us concentrate on its importance. Furthermore, all good relationships require communication. We listen and respond, but sometimes we respond with statements that focus on "what you do to me." When I express how I feel, I take the emphasis away from you. Exercise 17 deals with *I* statements. They allow for closeness and acceptance in relationships.

Exercise 14:
Looking at Your Relationship

AIM: To look at your relationship from both the positive and negative point of view.

PROCESS: During some quiet moments, reflect on your relationship, not in terms of the past, but how you see it presently. Rather than using general terms and one sentence, list all the positive aspects as you see them. List all of the negative aspects of the relationship. Rank the negative in terms of most to least crucial.

RESULTS: Do you work at maintaining the positive aspects? Has there been change? Are you able to change the negative aspects to something more positive? How? How are you able to improve other negative aspects of your relationship?

Exercise 15:
Focus on Passive Listening

AIM: To concentrate on the listening process.

PROCESS: Passive listening allows the person to talk with little interference from the listener. Be aware of this type of listening when a partner is anxious to talk about whatever happens to be on his/her mind. For example, it could be a certain situation at work. You simply listen, nod, or say "Tell me more" or "What else?" In many instances, the person does not expect you to solve anything. They simply want somebody to listen to them. Often, to be able to talk lowers the level of anxiety.

RESULTS: Note how difficult it might be not to interrupt or bring in, "you know what happened to me?" stories. Passive listening must be used appropriately. You will find, through experience, when people simply want you to *listen* and not respond.

Exercise 16:
Focus on Active Listening

AIM: To concentrate on the active listening process.

PROCESS: Active listening refers to the message beyond the words. For example, a person says, "I don't think I'll go to the party." You might reply, "Of course you should go!" Active listening refers to the emotional aspect related to the words. For example, is the underlying message one of fear, doubt, anger, frustration? For the above you might respond by saying, "You are afraid to . . .". Practice active listening when your partner makes statements, practice not only listening but tuning in to his/her feelings. Respond.

RESULTS: You will notice your partner says, "You understand my feelings," when you practice active listening. Do this with your friends. Practice makes perfect.

Exercise 17:
Using "I" Statements

AIM: To practice using *I* statements when communicating.

PROCESS: When communicating, we sometimes respond to our partners with *you* statements, such as, "You really annoy me!", "You make me angry!", etc. *You* statements are often put downs. They often denote some form of rejection with its accompanying emotions. During communication, practice the use of *I* statements such as, "I am always disappointed when . . ." or "I was angry when . . .". The *I* statement refers to your feelings about a situation; it is not meant to lower the self-esteem of your partner.

RESULTS: Does an *I* statement involve risk? How do you feel when you use the *I* statement? Do you notice any change in your partner's behavior when you omit *you* messages?

CONFLICT

I recall hearing one woman tell me that the first time she had a fight with her husband, she just about died. She never saw her parents in a situation where they were in conflict. I think this is a rare situation because the majority of relationships not only experience conflict but experience it quite frequently. Disagreement between two people does not signify a bad relationship, but how they react in conflict does matter. I would suggest that hitting a pillow is more healthy than suppressing anger or frustration.

However, conflict poses a danger which can be detrimental to any relationship if it is not handled properly from the beginning. The problem is that conflict signifies some degree of alienation between people. Furthermore, conflict feeds on itself until it reaches the point of explosion. Like fire, it must be handled with care before a situation becomes a raging inferno.

During conflict, adults usually behave like children. The net result is an angry shouting match except for one difference. Adults are unable to run home and tell mother (some probably do!). The confrontation becomes intense, filled with anger and, unfortunately, sometimes physical violence. The total situation is a sad state of affairs, because nothing is solved, actions are irrational, and partners end up hating each other. And yet I have seen the opposite form of punishment when one person will not speak to the other for three or four days. The silent treatment kills gently as well.

When conflicts arise, what can we do as sensible, human beings? As difficult as it may be, I would advise you to keep your cool and simply listen to what the other person is saying. This is one of the most important behavior patterns we can achieve. It is much easier said than done. To listen means to be in tune with the person's feelings. Usually the words by themselves do not convey much meaning. For example, "I'm fed up with housework!" may mean that the person would like to work outside the house rather than stay home and cook. The meaning behind the message must be understood. In addition, a person must learn to speak in specifics rather than generalities. "I hate phoning" is not as specific as "I hate to phone your mother!" And yet, how often we talk only in generalities. Often the reason a person avoids specifics is that his emotions are overriding the words. The net result is a language which is neither pleasant to hear nor easy to respond to.

We usually gain very little when we throw negative statements at each other and hit below the belt, so to speak. Emotions flare and words fly like bullets. During heated debates, we usually hear words such as *never* or *always* used rather frequently. For example, "you never listen to me!" is most often not true. It is next to impossible to never listen. Instead of screaming at another person we would usually be better off screaming at the mirror. The idea is that even if the mirror cracks, it is easier to buy a new one than it is to repair another person's feelings. We would be miles ahead if we could somehow listen to each other, take some sane action at attempting to hear what the other is saying. This is no easy task. Shouting at each other accomplishes nothing except exhaustion. Let us not act like children. If one can listen at least in part to the other's feelings, then the door opens ever so little to some positive action.

Is there any solution? Certainly most problems have a solution. However, one must look at the conflict in terms of what the underlying problem is and what the associated problems are. Along with this, you must consider what feelings emerge and what behavior patterns appear when the conflict comes into focus. What happens to you when you respond to the conflict? Does your partner react with fear, anger, or hurt? Regardless of the many facets of the conflict, you must think of the best solution for you and for your partner. Think of all the alternatives, weigh each one, and choose the course of action that is right for you. Like any other decision, you are never certain that you have the right answer, but only this can help you evaluate your life.

Exercises 18, 19, and 20 offer some approaches to dealing with conflict. The key is not to allow a relationship to deteriorate to the point that separation is the only answer.

Exercise 18:
Dealing with Emotions

AIM: To enable a partner to release his/her emotional feelings.

PROCESS: We often share happy feelings with sounds of laughter but crying is as healthy as laughing. We must not only learn to show our emotions but be supportive of others. During a situation when your partner is under some emotional distress, practice being a sympathetic, empathetic listener. Use eye contact. Give your attention. Let your partner focus on the hurt. Listen. Lend a supporting arm. Do not use any *you* or judgmental statements.

RESULTS: Do you feel uncomfortable in this situation? Why? What is most difficult to do? What can you do better? Does it work if you simply go through the motions? Why not?

Exercise 19:
Dealing with Emotions During Conflict

AIM: To allow emotions to be released during periods of conflict.

PROCESS: When shouting occurs in conflicts, very little is achieved by either person. Often two people express their anger at the same time. Emotions run high in conflicts. When your partner is showing anger, for example, allow him/her to release his emotion without any interruption on your part. Do not scream back at your partner. Do not be judgmental. Release your anger but not toward your partner. Cry if you want to. Both of you can learn this.

RESULTS: Since we tend to yell at each other under stress, releasing emotions can be handled differently, especially when conflicts first arise. Why is the process sometimes difficult to do? How do you feel? What does your partner experience? Is there any success in resolving your conflict? Is it important to release your emotions? Is there any other way?

Exercise 20:
Resolving Conflict

AIM: To examine various related aspects of a conflict and attempt some solutions.

PROCESS: Focus on the conflict in terms of the following:

A. *The Problem*
What is the problem?
How long has the problem existed?
What are the basic aspects of the problem?

B. *Individuals Involved*
How do the individuals respond in conflict?
What emotions do people express in the problem area?
Is the behavior pattern consistent?
What must change before effective solutions can be found?

C. *Decision*
How is each individual affected?
What are the alternatives?
What is the best solution?
What does each do for a successful outcome?
What are possible sources of interference?

D. *Solution*
Is the solution the best possible?
Is the solution difficult to implement?
What are the outcomes?

RESULTS: By using the various steps, which level is most difficult? Why? How do you know if you are successful in your decision? Solution? Can one situation apply to another? Why is it necessary to evaluate your solution?

LOOKING AHEAD

I feel that in our society too many relationships break down un-necessarily. People do not want to take the time to listen to each other or even find time to communicate feelings. I recently heard that the average couple spends about five minutes in serious conversation a week. If this is true, then we can see why there are very few, truly beautiful relationships. Maybe the majority of individuals deserve the relationship they have.

I also feel that many people do not try hard enough to resolve their differences. Maybe fleeing is a quick solution to some situations, but it may not be the best solution to all problems in relationships. Several couples I know recently celebrated their fiftieth wedding anniversaries. If they were starting their relationships in our present world, I think most of the couples would be lucky to have ten years together. Maybe individuals today have more choices, more options in their life to make decisions more easily. I admit that a bad relationship is worse than no relationship. However, I would like to see people try before they give up. The amount you try depends on who you are. Hopefully you know yourself better than others do.

I hope that you are able to perpetuate your relationship positively. As you and your partner continue to strive for greater closeness, your relationship will reach new heights. You continue to be individuals, but your love for each other continues to grow. There are very few feelings which hinder closeness. You practice active listening; you communicate openly.

Ideally, you do not spend all your time thinking about interest rates, mortgages, and profit. You think about yourself and your relationship. You continue to grow and to like who you are. You are a unique individual. You continue to be your best friend. You will never forsake yourself. From this firm base your relationship will grow to exciting levels. Loneliness will never stare into your eyes.

ten
Conclusion: Points of View

How can we talk about the brotherhood of man when we cannot wade through one day of news broadcasts without the mention of turmoil in this world? But why turn to the world, when we see brothers and sisters hurting each other, parents hurting their children, and children hurting their parents. I remember back in the 1940s when I was in elementary school, we had a teacher who had had little teacher training but who was blessed with a big heart. One day my classmate Sergei and I were in a wild fight. Punches, tears, groans, and shouting abounded as a circle of students witnessed the event. Somebody obviously told the teacher. She grabbed each of us by the collar and pulled us up from the dusty battle ground. "How can you expect the world to get along when you two, who should be friends, are punching each other out of existence?" she said. I remember that remark. It is not a profound statement, but it is so true. How can we expect the Middle East, Ireland, Africa, and countless other areas to live in peace, when we do not live in peace with our neighbors, our families, and with ourselves? We continue to seek undefined goals and act as if there were no tomorrow. We are lonely creatures on the surface of the globe. We seem to be in a hurry but we have no defined purpose in life.

Man has always been concerned about his state. Today, some worry about a better life hereafter, while others worry about a better life here on earth. Humanists for example, show a concern for man and for the development and expression of humanity. However, we must remember that humanity must first be thought of in terms of ourselves. When we think of humanism, we think of concepts such as self-image, self-esteem, and self-actualization. We attempt to strive toward the last goal common to all of us, that of self-actualization. We must not be satisfied with our sad state and attribute the situation to fate or bad luck. We have considerable control over our behavior. We were brought into this world with a set of genes. Some of us are better equipped than others. Some of us were buffeted by the world around us to such an extent that we cannot function without help. Some of us will probably never achieve great heights. The point is we try to the best of our abilities and circumstances. We move slowly along our own path of improvement which is not that of society as a whole.

Existentialism, which is very closely related to humanism, is concerned with man and his lonely state. Some philosophers describe this condition and believe that man's struggle is in vain, because when he dies, no one really cares. Other philosophers are concerned with man's state but also offer some solutions.

Jean-Paul Sartre and Martin Buber are two philosophers who not only contribute to the explanations of man's lonely state, but to my philosophy of life as well. Other philosophies could be discussed, because they also show concern for mankind. However, the problem is to further the state of well-being in man; to put theory into practice, whatever the theory may be. Buber's views emphasize the importance of love and the evil of alienation in this world. I agree with Buber's viewpoint; there is a need to experience love for self as well as for a selected group of others. Thus the existential, humanistic viewpoints have helped me to clarify certain values and goals in my life, and I try to the best of my ability to practice what I preach.

SARTRE'S VIEW

Jean-Paul Sartre looks at man's condition and describes him in terms of anguish, abandonment, and despair. Man is in anguish because he is always forced to make decisions in his lifetime, and he is never certain if the decisions he makes are correct. Man has few guidelines for making these decisions, and since he cannot rely on a higher power for help, he is faced with enormous responsibilities in his lifetime. Sartre also feels that man has not only been abandoned by other men, but he has also abandoned himself. He has little purpose and no definitive values. Man thinks he is free to make many choices and this has given him a high degree of freedom, but making these choices is not an easy task. Thus, the overall feeling is one of intense, indescribable loneliness. Man suffers from despair because even though he is free, he lacks hope. One can will something but not necessarily achieve it. An atheist, Sartre feels that what man does is meaningless, because everything disappears at death and the end is final.

One can perhaps agree with Sartre when he describes man's condition. However, not all people agree with the existential point of view. For example, if one believes in God then life is not in vain. I basically agree with Sartre that the overall state of man is not a happy one. Man does feel anguish, abandonment, and intense loneliness, but is he destined to live this way?

BUBER'S VIEW

Martin Buber takes a more optimistic view of mankind. He feels that man suffers from some of the evils of the modern world, but he also gives some solutions to the problems that face us. The first evil that plagues man is his terrible loneliness. As an existential philosopher, Buber is concerned with man's lonely condition and feels that the existence of the self is a lonely experience. The self only belongs to the individual and it cannot be completely shared with anyone else. This means that man is truly alone. In other words, man knows more about himself than any other person, and there are things he knows about himself that no other person knows or will ever know. The net result is loneliness.

Furthermore, Buber feels that there is a dichotomy between good and evil in man. I wonder about his observation. I would basically like to feel that man is essentially good, but I feel depressed when I hear what man does to his fellow man. How can men kill one another? How can man be so vicious? How is he able to snuff out the life of a child? How can man turn his back on a starving baby? How can man stare into the eyes of a lost soul? How can man watch with excitement the execution of another man? How can I believe that man is good, when people often wish the worst for other people? If man were at least neutral in his feelings then many of our world conflicts would be avoided. I wonder how man can so intensely want to achieve power, to conquer, and to be at the top.

Buber feels that the advance of technology is another evil that plagues man. As more and more machines take their place in man's world, his importance tends to decrease. We resent this, even though the machine can do the work faster and probably more efficiently. We find this to be the case in industry where machines work very effectively. Men who are involved in the world naturally feel inconsequential. The times are gone when a man spent his entire lifetime making a cathedral gate or carving a stone.

Finally, Buber feels that the state does little to enhance man. It reduces man to a faceless, nonentity rather than enhancing his uniqueness and self-worth. This is a feeling I have when I am in a large crowd. I ask myself, "Who am I in this mass of people?" As important as I think I may be, I feel like a nobody. How do I feel when I think in terms of millions of people? I feel like a number, a long number of punched slots on a card. In my own little environment, I feel more important. I hope that I am an asset, that I care, and that somebody in my world cares.

What is the overall result of the evils that plague man? He experiences loneliness compounded by alienation, alienation from the world, from people around him, and even from himself. Somehow the relationship that he should have with his private self may not exist. How can he have a relationship with others in the world? Is there no solution? Buber feels that as evil as alienation is, and as alienated as man feels, the opposite, and greatest good that man can possess is love, love for oneself and for others. Buber feels that man has hope and that the solution to his happiness and his struggle to attain greater heights can be achieved only through love.

It must be noted that Buber maintains that there is a need to love oneself as well as others. I feel very strongly that the former must precede the latter. One must feel that he has self-worth, that there is no one in the whole world that he would rather be. What about love for others? Buber describes love as an "I-Thou" relationship as compared to an "I-It" relationship. Let us examine what an "I-Thou" relationship entails. Buber speaks of a unity within a single man, between man and man, among nations and even the world. The "I-Thou" dialogue is an instrument to attain unity, as for example, between two people. In this relationship, the object or person is never used selfishly. One does not grow at the expense of the other person. The relationship is mutual. There is dialogue as opposed to monologue. One can say what he honestly means rather than what he feels is socially appropriate, or convenient at that moment.

MY PERSONAL PHILOSOPHY

Buber's definition of love as an "I-Thou" relationship is a significant contribution to the welfare of mankind. People talk about falling in and out of love; they speak of love, aging, or growing, but I really think they are not thinking of love in terms of the depth involved in Buber's definition. When you see a person and your knees turn to jelly, your heart pounds, and your forehead dampens, you think you are in love. I think you are infatuated. Love may be partly chemical but it does not happen overnight. For some people it may never happen.

There are people who are totally bored with each other; they merely exist. They are not in love. They are truly lonely and the forced smiles on their faces are only personified by the ulcers in their stomachs. How often does one person use another? How often are our conversations mere monologues? Do we not impatiently wait for our turn to speak, or even cut the other person off in our desperation to be heard? Do we really listen to the other person and accept him for what he is saying? What a beautiful job we do covering up for the next person. How often I hear women covering up for their husbands; pretending they are okay, great, and almost convincing themselves. They say what is socially appropriate and not what they feel in their hearts. How will these women be able to express their fear of being hurt and rejected? Is this love? How can loneliness be overcome in this situation?

Diametrically opposed to the "I-Thou" relationship is the "I-It" relationship which is a monologue. It is one-sided, relating to man's physical and empirical world, to the world of things we use and experience. It reflects an attitude that views people as objects. This type of relationship, devoid of sharing and communion, breeds loneliness. The relationship produces not only children, material goods, and artificial happiness, but also emptiness. Unfortunately, "I-It" relationships do exist in the world around us.

Love is not a subjective feeling buried inside individuals; rather, it connects them. When a man and woman fall in love, love exists between them. Feelings dwell in man and woman, but man and woman dwell in love. Love does not cling to the "I." Love lies between "I" and "Thou." The man who is ignorant of this does not know love. So it is with all human relationships. The real substance of our world is what exists between two people. The attitude is either "I-Thou" with mutuality and communion or one of "I-It" accompanied by nothingness.

Epilogue

And the days come and go. Winter snows give way to the warm days of summer. Flowers and green grass give way to the colored leaves of autumn. There is sadness in the air and I feel melancholy. But this season always makes me think of the rewards for man's work; for some there is very little to reap. They can only think of the cold wind that will be replacing the warmth of the sun. There is loneliness, intense loneliness.

I look up. The sky is very blue. And I look at that cloud! It seems as though someone took a huge brush and made a long sweep across the sky. Isn't it beautiful? I stare at it; the color changes from a deep red to a soft pink. I look again and evening begins to darken the sky. I think. Is there hope for me? Am I destined to be a lonely creature pursuing colorless rainbows all my life?

I live through the experience and I grow. I must dwell in myself and grow as a human being. I must reach out. I am a man with all my strengths, weaknesses, beauty, and ugliness. Yes, I can grow and some day I may be able to laugh, cry, and feel. I will leave my silent company. The room darkens and I fall into a deep sleep.

References

BRAIN, R. Somebody else should be your own best friend. *Psychology Today,* October 1977, p. 83.

BRYANT, C. (Ed.). New light on adult life cycles. *Time,* April 28, 1975, p. 43.

BUBER, M. *I and Thou.* New York: Charles Scribner's Sons, 1958.

DIEHL, D. Looking at forty. *Esquire,* March 1981, pp. 25–38.

GOBLE, F.G. *The Third Force.* New York: Grossman, 1970.

HAMACHEK, D.E. *Encounters with the Self.* New York: Holt, Rinehart & Winston, 1970.

HAMACHEK, D.E. *Behavior Dynamics in Teaching, Learning and Growth.* Boston: Allyn & Bacon, Inc., 1975.

MAEIR, H.W. The psychoanalytic theory of Erik H. Erikson. In *Three Theories of Child Development.* New York: Harper & Row Publishers, Inc., 1965, pp. 12–75.

MASLOW, A. *Toward a Psychology of Being.* Princeton, N.J.: D. Van Nostrand Co., 1968.

MASLOW, A.H. A theory of motivation. In R.F. Biehler (Ed.), *Psychology Applied to Teaching.* Boston: Houghton Mifflin Co., 1972, pp. 338–362.

MEYERSON, S. (Ed.). *Adolescence and Breakdown.* London: George Allen & Unwin Ltd., 1975.

MITCHELL, J.J. *Adolescence. Some Critical Issues.* Toronto: Holt, Rinehart & Winston of Canada Ltd., 1971.

MOOD, J.L. *Rilke on Love and Other Difficulties.* New York: W.W. Norton & Co., Inc., 1975.

MOSSE, E.P. *The Conquest of Loneliness.* New York: Random House Inc., 1957.

MOUSTAKAS, C.E. *Loneliness and Love.* Englewood Cliffs, N.J.: Prentice-Hall, Inc., 1961.

MOUSTAKAS, C.E. *Loneliness and Love.* Englewood Cliffs, N.J.: Prentice-Hall, Inc., 1972.

MURDOCK, I. *Sartre.* Glasgow: W. Collins & Co., April, 1976.

TERKEL, S. *Working.* New York: Avon Books, 1975.

TILLICH, P. *The Courage to Be.* New Haven, Conn.: Yale University Press, 1952.

WARNOCK, M. *Existentialism.* Oxford: Oxford University Press, 1970.

WINSTEIN, J. *Buber and Humanistic Education.* New York: Philosophical Society Library, 1975.

WEISS, R.S. *Loneliness.* Cambridge: The M.I.T. Press, 1973.

ZILLER, R.C. *The Social Self.* Toronto: Pergamon Press, Inc., 1973.

ZWELL, M. *How to Succeed at Love.* Englewood Cliffs, N.J.: Prentice-Hall, Inc., 1978.

Index